Speak NOW 1

COMMUNICATE with CONFIDENCE

WORKBOOK

OXFORD
UNIVERSITY PRESS

OXFORD
UNIVERSITY PRESS

198 Madison Avenue
New York, NY 10016 USA

Great Clarendon Street, Oxford, OX2 6DP, United Kingdom

Oxford University Press is a department of the University of Oxford.
It furthers the University's objective of excellence in research, scholarship,
and education by publishing worldwide. Oxford is a registered trade
mark of Oxford University Press in the UK and in certain other countries

© Oxford University Press 2013

The moral rights of the author have been asserted

First published in 2013

2017 2016 2015 2014 2013
10 9 8 7 6 5 4 3 2

No unauthorized photocopying

All rights reserved. No part of this publication may be reproduced, stored
in a retrieval system, or transmitted, in any form or by any means, without
the prior permission in writing of Oxford University Press, or as expressly
permitted by law, by licence or under terms agreed with the appropriate
reprographics rights organization. Enquiries concerning reproduction outside
the scope of the above should be sent to the ELT Rights Department, Oxford
University Press, at the address above

You must not circulate this work in any other form and you must impose
this same condition on any acquirer

Links to third party websites are provided by Oxford in good faith and for
information only. Oxford disclaims any responsibility for the materials
contained in any third party website referenced in this work

General Manager, American ELT: Laura Pearson
Executive Publishing Manager: Erik Gundersen
Managing Editor: Jennifer Meldrum
Associate Editor: Tristan Child
Director, ADP: Susan Sanguily
Executive Design Manager: Maj-Britt Hagsted
Associate Design Manager: Michael Steinhofer
Image Manager: Trisha Masterson
Art Editor: Joe Kassner
Electronic Production Manager: Julie Armstrong
Production Artist: Elissa Santos
Production Coordinator: Brad Tucker

ISBN: 978 0 19 403052 6   WORKBOOK

Printed in China

This book is printed on paper from certified and well-managed sources

ACKNOWLEDGEMENTS

Cover Design: Molly K. Scanlon

Illustrations by: Barb Bastian, Kenneth Batelman, Kun-Sung Chung,
Bunky Hurter, Javier Joaquin, Joe LeMonnier, Gavin Reece, Heidi Schmidt,
Rob Schuster.

Contents

	THEMES	SKILLS	PAGES
Lessons 1–4	NEW FRIENDS	Vocabulary	1, 3, 5, 7
		Reading and Writing	2, 4, 6, 8
		Video Comprehension	9
		Grammar	10, 11, 12
Lessons 5–8	INTERESTS	Vocabulary	13, 15, 17, 19
		Reading and Writing	14, 16, 18, 20
		Video Comprehension	21
		Grammar	22, 23, 24
Lessons 9–12	PEOPLE	Vocabulary	25, 27, 29, 31
		Reading and Writing	26, 28, 30, 32
		Video Comprehension	33
		Grammar	34, 35
Lessons 13–16	DAILY LIFE	Vocabulary	36, 38, 40, 42
		Reading and Writing	37, 39, 41, 43
		Video Comprehension	44
		Grammar	45, 46
Lessons 17–20	MY HOMETOWN	Vocabulary	47, 49, 51, 53
		Reading and Writing	48, 50, 52, 54
		Video Comprehension	55
		Grammar	56, 57, 58, 59
Lessons 21–24	SHOPPING	Vocabulary	60, 62, 64, 66
		Reading and Writing	61, 63, 65, 67
		Video Comprehension	68
		Grammar	69, 70
Lessons 25–28	FOOD	Vocabulary	71, 73, 75, 77
		Reading and Writing	72, 74, 76, 78
		Video Comprehension	79
		Grammar	80
Lessons 29–32	PAST & FUTURE	Vocabulary	81, 83, 85, 87
		Reading and Writing	82, 84, 86, 88
		Video Comprehension	89
		Grammar	90, 91

Lesson 1: Vocabulary

NEW FRIENDS

Part 1

Complete the conversation with your own answers. In class, practice the conversations with a partner.

New teacher: Hi! What's your first name?
You: _____

New teacher: And what's your last name?
You: _____

New teacher: What's your middle name?
You: _____

New teacher: Great. Thanks. It's nice to meet you.

Part 2

Choose the best word or phrase to complete each conversation. In class, practice the conversations with a partner.

1.
Yuko: (Hi, Mao. / How are you doing, Mao?)
Mao: Fine, thanks.
Yuko: Oh, my train is here.
Mao: (Fine, thanks. / OK. Good night.)

2.
Ms. Anders: (Hey / Hello), Ms. Kim.
Ms. Kim: How is everything?
Ms. Anders: Everything is great, thank you. How are you?
Ms. Kim: (Good. / I'm fine, thank you.)

3.
Francis: Hi, Andy. How are things?
Andy: I'm all right. You?
Francis: (Not bad. / I'm fine, thank you.)

4.
Melissa: (Good night / Goodbye), Professor Ramos.
Ms. Ramos: Goodbye, Melissa.

Lesson 1: Reading & Writing

NEW FRIENDS

Part 1

Read the letter below.

University of America
Where every student is special.

3256 22nd Street
Minneapolis, Minnesota 55416
800-852-7946

Ms. Renee Maria Smith
254 Larry Lane
St. Petersburg, Florida 33701-4313
April 29, 2013

Dear Ms. Smith,

Congratulations! It is my pleasure to tell you that you have been accepted to University of America. To keep your place in the University of America's class entering August 2013 and graduating May 2017, please fill in the form and send it to us.

Again, let me say congratulations. I wish you the best in your studies at University of America.

Sincerely,

Mr. Andre Fiori
Director of Admissions

Complete the sentences.

1. Her first name is _____.
2. Her middle name is _____.
3. Her last name is _____.
4. This is a formal _____.
5. The last name of the Director of Admissions is _____.

PAIR WORK Discuss the questions.

In your country, is it difficult to get into university? Do most people want to go to university? Give reasons for your answers.

Part 2

Write a short, formal letter to Mr. Fiori. Tell him you are happy you can go to his university.

Part 3

In a group, share what you have written to Mr. Fiori. What are some different reasons why your classmates are happy about attending his university?

Lesson 2: Vocabulary

NEW FRIENDS

Part 1

Match the words from the box to their definitions.

| classmate | teacher | friend | neighbor | relative | colleague | boss | stranger |

1. A person you work with is a _____.
2. Someone you don't know at all is a _____.
3. Someone who lives near you is a _____.
4. One of the people you study with is a _____.
5. The person who tells you what to do at your job is your _____.
6. The person who helps you learn in class is your _____.
7. A person such as your mother's mother is a _____.
8. Someone you like to spend time with is a _____.

Part 2

How often do you see the people in Part 1? Put them in order from most often to least often. In class, talk about your ideas with a partner.

_____

_____

Part 3

Write the words from Part 1 to complete the first sentence in each conversation. Then write what the second person says. In class, practice the conversations with a partner.

1.

Yukiko: Excuse me, Ralph. This is my _____. We work together at Oxford University Press.

Ralph: _____

2.

YeQuing: Hi, Bak. I'd like you to meet my _____. We first met 10 years ago.

Bak: _____

3.

Inger: Hi. I'm Inger, and this is my _____. I live in 4A, and he lives in 5B.

David: _____

Lesson 2: Reading & Writing

FRIENDS & FAMILY

Part 1

Read the application.

Homestay Application

YOU First Name: __Qing__   Middle Name: __(none)__   Last name: __Zhao__
Birthday: __January 15, 1993__   Age: __20__   Gender: (M) F
Grade in school: __3rd year of university__
Where are you from? __China__
I __have__ been to another country. (Where?
__I went to Australia.__ How long? __I went for one week.__ Who with?
__I went with my family.__)
Your English Where do you study English? __my university__
When did you start to study English? __elementary school__
Do you like English? __Yes, I love it.__
Homestay Alone? __No__   Other students in the house? __Yes__
I want to live in __London or Yorkshire in the U.K.__
Program: __3 months__
I heard about this program from __a teacher and my friend.__

Mark the statements **T** (True) or **F** (False).

_____ 1. His name is Qing Zhao.

_____ 2. Qing is from Yorkshire.

_____ 3. Qing wants to live with other students.

_____ 4. Qing loves English.

_____ 5. Qing wants to go to Australia.

_____ 6. Qing wants to go to another country for 13 months.

 **PAIR WORK** With a partner, correct the false statements.

Part 2

Imagine you want to have a homestay in an English-speaking country. Write sentences to introduce yourself. Include the same kind of information as the above application.

Part 3

In class, compare your reasons for wanting to participate in a homestay program with your classmates' reasons.

Lesson 3: Vocabulary

NEW FRIENDS

Part 1
Write one or two words to complete each way of communicating. If a word is not needed, write an X.

1. _____ an e-mail
2. _____ a text
3. _____ in person
4. _____ instant message
5. _____ video chat
6. _____ social network
7. _____ a letter
8. _____ on the phone

Part 2
Do you do each activity in Part 1 alone, with another person, or sometimes alone and sometimes with another person? Write each activity in the correct place in the diagram.

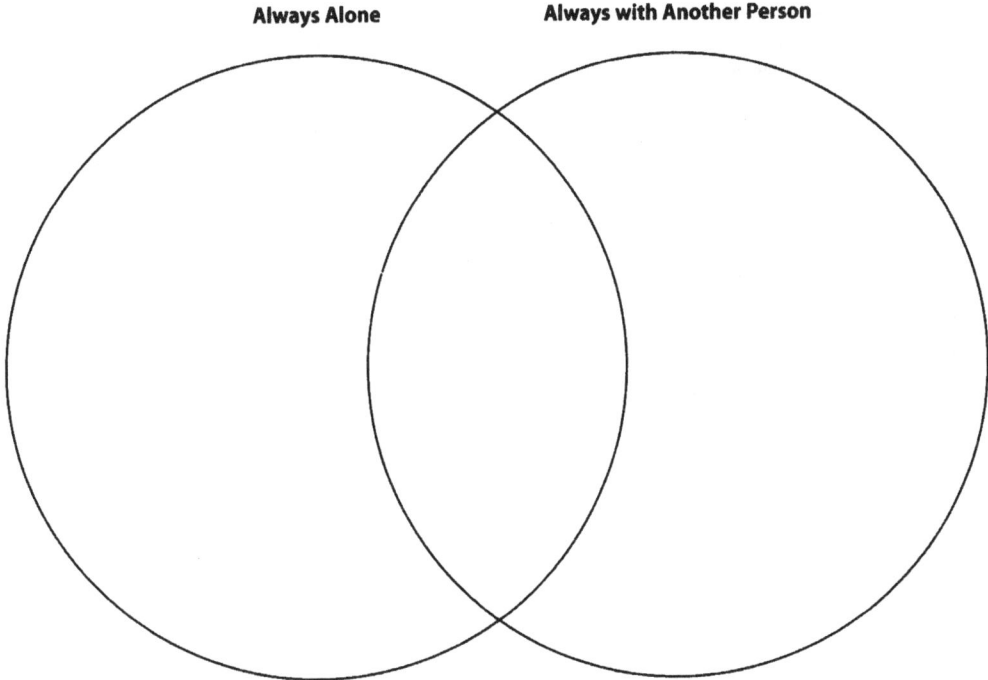

Always Alone   **Always with Another Person**

In class, compare answers with a partner.

A: I usually write an e-mail alone. How about you?
B: I do, too.

Lesson 3: Reading & Writing

NEW FRIENDS

Part 1

Read the class description below.

Communication 101

Professor Ahmad
Education Building, Room 423
Tuesdays and Thursdays 8:30-10 p.m.
Open to all students

How do you communicate with people? Do you write a letter or an e-mail? Do you send a text or talk on the phone? Do you like to meet in person or chat with video? Is there one way of communication that is better than another?

In this class, we will talk about how we communicate, and we will talk about how people of different ages and in different situations communicate in different ways. We will also look at how communication has changed in the last 100 years.

Answer the questions.

1. Who is teaching the class? _____
2. How many hours a week does the class meet? _____
3. What is the name of the class? _____
4. What changes will the students study? _____
5. Who can take this class? _____

PAIR WORK Discuss the questions.

1. Do you want to take this class? Give reasons for your answer.
2. What classes are you taking now?
3. What kind of classes do you like to take?
4. Are classes a good way to meet new people? Why?

Part 2

Image you are going to make a weekly chat time so new students can meet each other. Will there be food? When and where will it meet? Who can come? Write a description like the one above.

Part 3

Share your weekly chat ideas with a partner. Talk about other ways new students can meet each other.

Lesson 4: Vocabulary

NEW FRIENDS

Part 1

How often do you talk about these things? Put them in order from 1 (most often) to 8 (least often, never). Who do you talk with? Write your answer on the second line.

In class, talk about your ideas with a partner.

_____ school _____   _____ movies _____

_____ family _____   _____ hobbies _____

_____ music _____   _____ money _____

_____ sports _____   _____ TV shows _____

Part 2

Check (✓) the sentences and questions you might use to make small talk.

_____ It's really beautiful today, isn't it?

_____ It really is.

_____ This sunny weather is great, isn't it?

_____ How old are you?

_____ Yeah, this cloudy weather sure is terrible.

_____ How's school/work?

_____ Hot/cold, huh?

_____ What's your middle name?

_____ I'm really busy these days. You?

Part 3

Use some of the sentences and questions in Part 2 to make two short conversations. Practice them with a partner in class.

1.

You: _____

Partner: _____

2.

You: _____

Partner: _____

Lesson 4: Reading & Writing

NEW FRIENDS

Part 1

Read the postcard.

Hello from Brazil!

April 5, 2013

Dear Sansfica,

I'm having a great time in São Paulo. It's really nice today—sunny and warm. But yesterday it was cloudy and a little cold.

I started staying with my host family last night. In total, I'll stay with them for three nights. They have a daughter, Manu, who is the same age as me. I was worried, but they all speak great English. We talked about music and movies, and we even like the same ones!

How are things at school? If you have time, we can video chat next weekend. I want to hear how everyone is.

The month will be over before I know it!

Leah

Sansfica Salazar
1785 Old Maple Lane
Hollywood, CA 72013
AIR MAIL

Write the correct word(s) to complete the sentences.

1. _____ is in Brazil right now.
2. She's staying with her host family for _____ more nights.
3. Leah and _____ are the same age.
4. On April 4, the weather was _____.
5. Leah is going to be gone for _____.

PAIR WORK Discuss the questions.

1. When do most people write postcards, and to whom do they send them?
2. Do we need to make small talk when we write postcards? Give reasons for your answer.
3. What kinds of personal information should you not write on a postcard?

Part 2

Imagine you are Sansfica. Write a postcard to Leah. Talk about the weather and a new friend at school.

Part 3

Read your postcard to a partner without telling them where you are visiting. Have them guess where you are writing about.

Lessons 1-4: Video Cloze

NEW FRIENDS

Watch *New Neighbors* and fill in the blanks.

Eric: Hi.

Jill: Hello. Sorry to bother you. My friend and I are new to the building. We're in ____(1)____ 3F.

Eric: Oh, welcome to the building!

Jill: I hate to ask, but do you have a broom?

Eric: A broom? Oh, sure. Tom, where is our broom?

Tom: Hold on.

Eric: Please, please, come inside.

Jill: Thanks. By the way, my ____(2)____ Jill.

Eric: I'm Eric. And this is my friend and roommate, Tom.

Tom: Here you go.

Jill: Thanks. Oh, are you new to the ____(3)____, too?

Tom: Um, no. Why?

Jill: Oh, never mind.

Maria: Jill?

Jill: I'm in here. Come and meet our ____(4)____. This is Tom and this is Eric. This is my ____(5)____, Maria.

Maria: ____(6)____. How's it ____(7)____?

Tom: Not bad.

Eric: ____(8)____ good.

Tom: Excuse me for a minute.

Jill: That smells good. What's for ____(9)____?

Tom: I'm not sure yet. But right now, it's tomato sauce.

Eric: It's pasta and tomato sauce. He *always* makes pasta!

Tom: I do not! Hey, I have an idea. Stay and have some with us.

Maria: Oh, um, but we need to clean our apartment.

Tom: Come ____(10)____ in about 30 minutes.

Jill: Are you sure? That's really ____(11)____ of you.

Maria: Yeah. Our refrigerator is empty.

Eric: I'll text you when it's ready. Can I get your ____(12)____?

Jill: Sure. It's 555-3992.

Eric: I'm sorry. Can you ____(13)____ that?

Jill: 555-3992.

Eric: Got it.

Maria: Thanks, guys. We'll see you ____(14)____.

Jill: Bye.

Eric: See you ____(15)____.

Tom: Bye! I hope you're hungry!

Tom: Hm...What should I make?

Eric: Aha!

Tom: What? I like pasta. Eric? Will you ask Jill to bring the broom?

Lessons 1-4: Grammar A

NEW FRIENDS

Contractions

Full form	Contraction
I am	I'm
You are	You're
He is	He's
She is	She's
It is	It's
We are	We're
My name is	My name's
What is	What's
Who is	Who's
How is	How's
Is not	Isn't
Do not	Don't
Does not	Doesn't

Part 1

Circle the contractions in the sentence. Then write the full form.

1. I (don't) like watching TV. _____do not_____
2. What's his name? _____
3. I'm a teacher. _____
4. We're in the same class. _____
5. Who's your teacher? _____
6. It's a beautiful day. _____

Part 2

Rewrite the sentences using contractions

1. How is it going? _____How's it going?_____
2. Mike does not like chocolate. _____
3. My name is Walter. _____
4. She is a teacher. _____
5. He is not a student. _____
6. We do not have a test today. _____

Lessons 1-4: Grammar B

NEW FRIENDS

Tag questions

> **Tag questions...**
> are added at the end of a sentence.
> turn statements into questions.
> are usually used by speakers to check their information or to gain agreement.
>
> **Affirmative sentence + negative tag** (affirmative answer expected)
>
> Sarah: The weather's beautiful, isn't it?
> Karina: Yes, it is.
> Sarah: You have a lot of friends, don't you?
> Karina: Yes, I do.
>
> **Negative sentence + affirmative tag** (negative answer expected)
>
> Mike: This movie isn't very good, is it?
> Jim: No, it isn't.
> Mike: You don't have any money, do you?
> Jim: No, I don't.

Part 1

Complete the conversations. Write the tag questions.

1. A: This café is crowded, _____isn't it_____ ? B: Yes, it is.
2. A: Lara doesn't live near the school, _____ ? B: No, she doesn't.
3. A: The teacher is nice, _____ ? B: Yes, she is.
4. A: We don't have a lot of homework, _____ ? B: No, we don't.
5. A: Mike's brother studies hard, _____ ? B: Yes, he does.
6. A: The bus wasn't crowded this morning, _____ ? B: No, it wasn't.

Part 2

Complete the conversations. Write the tag questions.

1. A: It's nice today, isn't it? B: _____Yes, it is._____ .
2. A: The test wasn't easy, was it? B: _____ .
3. A: They like ice cream, don't they? B: _____ .
4. A: You walk to school, don't you? B: _____ .
5. A: Sara doesn't have a car, does she? B: _____ .
6. A: The homework isn't too hard, is it? B: _____ .

Lessons 1-4: Grammar C

NEW FRIENDS

Polite requests

> **You can use *I'd like* + an infinitive to make a polite request:**
>
> I want a job application. → **I'd like** to have a job application.
>
> **You can also use *May I / Could I / Can I* + a verb to make a polite request:**
>
> **May I** have a job application?
> I want a job application. → **Could I** have a job application?
> **Can I** have a job application?
>
> **Add *please* to make requests more polite:**
>
> With *May I*, *Could I*, and *Can I*, you can add **please** before the verb, or at the beginning or the end of the sentence. (Notice the comma.)
>
> May I **please** have a job application?
> **Please** may I have a job application?
> May I have a job application, **please**?
>
> With *I'd like*, you can only add **please** at the end. (Notice the comma.)
>
> I'd like a job application, **please**.

Part 1

Complete the sentences. Write the correct form of the verb.

1. May I ____*borrow*____ a pen?
   (borrow)
2. I'd like _____ here.
   (sit)
3. Could I _____ a window?
   (open)
4. I'd like _____ a glass of water.
   (have)
5. Can I _____ a question?
   (ask)
6. I'd like _____ now.
   (go)

Part 2

Write *please* in the correct place, a or b. Add a comma, if necessary.

1. May _____ I _____ have a salad?
       (a)   (b)
2. Can I come _____ with you _____?
              (a)   (b)
3. I'd _____ like to speak with you _____.
      (a)   (b)
4. Could I _____ use _____ your phone?
           (a)   (b)
5. _____ I'd like to get some help _____.
   (a)   (b)
6. I'd like _____ to make an appointment _____.
            (a)   (b)

Lesson 5: Vocabulary

INTERESTS

Part 1

Do you like this music? Write I love [the music] (☺☺), I like [the music] (☺), I don't really like [the music] (☹), or I don't like [the music] at all (☹☹).

1. rock _____ I don't really like rock. _____
2. pop _____
3. country _____
4. hip-hop _____
5. classical _____
6. jazz _____
7. folk _____
8. techno _____
9. heavy metal _____
10. reggae _____

In class, compare answers with a partner. Do you like the same music or different music?

A: I don't really like rock music. Do you?
B: I love it!

Part 2

In each of B's answers, one word is wrong. Cross it out and write the correct word on the line. In class, practice the correct conversations with your partner.

1. A: I love techno.
   B: Really? I ~~do~~. _____don't_____

2. A: I don't like jazz at all.
   B: Either do I. _____

3. A: I like reggae.
   B: Me neither. _____

4. A: I really like country.
   B: Neither do I. _____

5. A: I don't really like hip-hop.
   B: Oh, I don't. _____

6. A: I really dislike heavy metal.
   B: Really? I do. _____

Part 3

Look at the conversations in Part 2. Do A and B like the same (S) music or different (D) music?

1. _____
2. _____
3. _____
4. _____
5. _____
6. _____

Lesson 5: Reading & Writing

INTERESTS

Part 1

Read the newspaper article below.

Friday Night Concerts

Summer is almost here, and that means the start of the Friday Night Concerts in the Park series. Every Friday through August, you can hear a different group—for free. This year is the 21st year of the series, and the concerts are always popular.

- May 3   Smooth sounds with horns and piano.
- May 10   Beware! This band will get your heart pumping.
- May 17   An orchestra that people of all ages love.
- May 24   Dance your way through an evening of fun.
- May 31   This concert may not be for everyone. Loud, with a good beat.

All concerts start at 8 p.m. For more information and other schedules, contact Concerts in the Park at 308-712-9645 or ConcertsInPark.org.

Match the type of music to the date.

_____ 1. May 3   a. classical

_____ 2. May 10   b. techno

_____ 3. May 17   c. heavy metal

_____ 4. May 24   d. hip-hop

_____ 5. May 31   e. jazz

 **PAIR WORK** Discuss the questions.

1. What important information is missing from the newspaper article?
2. Which concerts are you interested in going to?
3. What kinds of people probably go to free concerts in the park?
4. What are some good and bad things about free concerts in the park?

Part 2

Write a newspaper article about an event taking place in your town.

Part 3

Share your event with a partner. Ask if they will attend and why.

Lesson 6: Vocabulary

INTERESTS

Part 1

Rank these interests from 1 (most interesting for you) to 8 (not at all interesting to you). Then write three words about that interest.

In class, talk about your ideas with a partner.

1. _____ movies
   _____actor, actress, Emma Watson_____

2. _____ sports
   _____

3. _____ food
   _____

4. _____ video games
   _____

5. _____ music
   _____

6. _____ books
   _____

7. _____ shopping
   _____

8. _____ travel
   _____

Part 2

Use your ideas from Part 1 and other ideas to complete the conversation. In class, get into groups of three and practice it.

You: What's your favorite movie?
Partner 1:   1. _____My favorite movie is_____.
Partner 2:   I like 2. _____.
Partner 1:   How about actors and actresses? Who's your favorite actress?
You: I'm crazy about 3. _____.
Partner 1:   Really? 4. _____.
Partner 2:   And what about music? What's your favorite song?
You: 5. _____.
Partner 2:   So you like 6. _____?
You: 7. _____.
Partner 1:   Well, what about video games? Do you like any games in particular?
You: 8. _____.

Lesson 6: Reading & Writing

INTERESTS

Part 1

Read the magazine article.

> **Most popular travel movie 2003-2013**
>
> Every ten years I have to decide on the top travel movie of the past decade. It's not easy to choose just one, so here are my top two.
>
> **Number 1: Peru Journey**
>
> This movie came out nine years ago, but every time I see it, it makes me want to go to Peru. The information is interesting, and the scenes of Peru are amazing. I particularly like the scenes of Machu Picchu. One of the bad things about the movie is that it is three hours long. Have some snacks before you start it!
>
> **Number 2: Across Africa**
>
> This movie came out last year, but it isn't your usual travel movie. It's the story about how one family traveled across Africa. It took them four years, and during that time, there were many problems. The music is amazing, but the acting could be better.

Complete the sentences.

1. In the first paragraph, the word *decade* means _____.
2. The movie about Peru came out in _____.
3. The good thing about the second movie is _____.
4. The good points about the first movie are _____ and _____.
5. The bad point about the second movie is _____.

PAIR WORK Discuss the questions.

1. Do you want to see the movies? Give reasons for your answer.
2. Is there any other information you want to know about each movie?
3. What was the best movie you saw last year? Give reasons for your answer.

Part 2

Write a review of a movie. Include what you liked and didn't like about the movie.

Part 3

In class, share your review and talk about what kinds of movies you like and don't like. Make a list of the top five movies you want to see that were reviewed by your classmates.

Lesson 7: Vocabulary

INTERESTS

Part 1

What time is it? Draw clocks.

It's half past eleven.

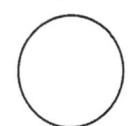

It's five to four.

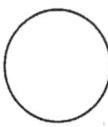

It's a quarter after one.

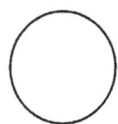

It's a quarter to nine.

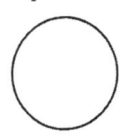

It's noon.

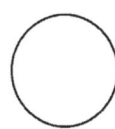

It's midnight.

Part 2

What time is it? Write your answers in words. Use *after* and *to*.

1. 10:05 _____
2. 3:10 _____
3. 8:20 _____
4. 6:25 _____
5. 7:40 _____
6. 5:50 _____
7. 1:35 _____

Part 3

Look at your schedule. Answer the questions using words.

Monday	
10:30	English class
1:00	Work
7:30	Birthday party

1. What time is your English class? _____
2. What time is your job? _____
3. What time is the birthday party? _____

Lesson 7: Reading & Writing

INTERESTS

Part 1

Read the timetables.

Train Service April-June		
Leave Barcelona	**Arrive Madrid**	**Days of Service**
six thirty a.m.	nine fifteen a.m.	M-F
six forty-five a.m.	nine thirty a.m.	Sat, Sun
nine forty-five a.m.	twelve thirty p.m.	T, Th

Flight Schedule April-June			
Leave Singapore	**From**	**Arrive Bangkok**	**Flight Number**
seven thirty a.m.	Gate 44C	eight fifteen a.m.	482
eight thirty a.m.	Gate 44B	nine fifteen a.m.	484
nine forty-five a.m.	Gate 44A	ten fifteen a.m.	486

Memo

Susan,
Please buy a train ticket for George Colbert to go to Madrid on Saturday. Please also get a ticket for me to fly to Bangkok. I need to get there between 9 and 10 in the morning.
Thanks,
Greg

Complete the information about George and Greg's travel.

George: Day: _____ Leave: _____ Travel time: _____

Greg: Flight Number: _____ Gate: _____

Leave: _____ Travel time: _____ Arrive: _____

Part 2

Create a timetable for a train like the one above using two cities from your country. Include Leave times, Arrive times, and Days of Service.

Part 3

Show your timetable to a partner. Have them buy a ticket from you. Take turns asking and answering questions about the times and days of service.

Lesson 8: Vocabulary

INTERESTS

Part 1

Which word is different? Circle it. In class, talk about why it is different with a partner.

1. dangerous   hard   golf
2. soccer   baseball   bungee jumping
3. kayaking   interesting   challenging
4. rock climbing   skydiving   wrestling
5. exciting   boring   fun
6. snowboarding   skateboarding   boxing
7. surfing   jet skiing   soccer

Part 2

Complete the conversation with your own answers. Practice it with a partner in class.

Friend: What do you think about jet skiing?

You: I think it's _____

Friend: Really? I think _____

Part 3

Use the words from Part 1 to write the opposites.

exciting _____   safe _____   easy _____

Part 4

Do you use a ball to do the activities in Part 1? Do you do them inside? Are they dangerous? Write the activities in the diagram below. In class, compare answers with a partner.

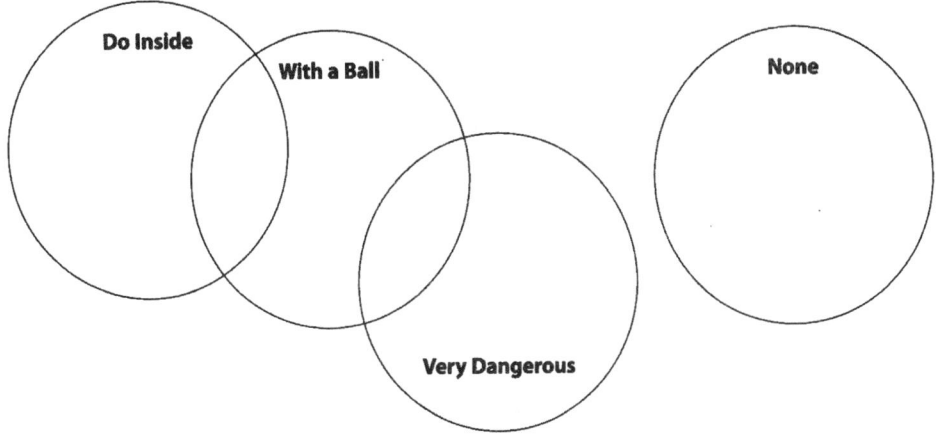

Lesson 8: Reading & Writing

INTERESTS

Part 1

Read the advertisement below.

Would you try jet skiing?
Then take this safety course first.

There are safety courses throughout the country, for people of all ages and skills. This course is important because 10% of all boaters use jet skis. Each course includes topics like:

- Watching the weather
- The water and children
- In and out of the water safety
- Checking your jet ski before you use it

Most courses are six to ten lessons of two to three hours each.
Look for courses with a state approval because they met the standards of the National Association of State Boating Law Administrators.
Contact your state recreation department for more information.
California Safe Boating Department

Answer the questions.
1. Who is this advertisement for? _____
2. How long is the shortest course? _____
3. Who put this advertisement in the magazine? _____
4. According to the advertisement, do people who have jet skied need to take this course? _____
5. According to the advertisement, which safety courses are best to take? _____

 **PAIR WORK** Discuss the questions.

Why is it important to take safety courses before trying adventure sports? What other sports probably have safety courses?

Part 2

Imagine you want to take a jet ski safety course with your friend. Write an e-mail telling him/her about the course and why you should take it.

Part 3

Get into pairs. Pretend you don't want to take the course and have your friend tell you why it's important.

Lessons 5-8: Video Cloze

INTERESTS

Watch *A Birthday Present* and fill in the blanks.

Maria: I don't know what to get Jill for her birthday.
Tom: Hm... how about a ticket to a baseball game?
Maria: Jill doesn't like baseball at all. Actually, she doesn't like any _____ (1).
Tom: Really? I love sports! Well, what does she like?
Maria: She likes music.
Tom: What kind?
Maria: She loves hip-hop and _____ (2) _____ (3).
Tom: Heavy metal?! Oh, I don't like heavy metal.
Maria: Me neither. I think it's too loud.
Tom: Who's her favorite _____ (4)?
Maria: Well, her _____ (5) hip-hop artist is Kanye West.
Tom: Me too! What about you?
Maria: I don't really like _____ (6).
Tom: Well, do you like any _____ (7) in particular?
Maria: I like Coldplay.
Tom: So do I! I have all their CDs. Hey, what do you think of getting her a CD?
Maria: Jill never buys CDs. She _____ (8) all her music.
Tom: Why don't you get her tickets to a concert?
Maria: That's a good idea.
Tom: Let's look online.
Tom: Here's something. Susannah Mason. What do you think of her?

Maria: The folk singer? I think she's great, but Jill doesn't like _____ (9) music.
Tom: How about this? Hip-Hop Madness. It's tomorrow night. _____ (10) are $35.
Maria: It doesn't sound interesting to me.
Tom: It sounds fun to me! It's at 8:00. Doors open at _____ (11) _____ (12) seven.
Maria: Let's look for something else.
Maria: Hey, what about this? Tickets to the new _____ (13) Dance City!
Tom: I heard it was really good!
Maria: Jill loves musicals!
Tom: Perfect! Buy four tickets. It starts at 7:30, so we can meet at 7:00.
Maria: I'm buying them now.
Eric: Hi, guys.
Tom: Hi, Eric. How was _____ (14) class?
Eric: It was great. Math is my favorite subject.
Tom: Is there any subject you don't like?
Eric: No, of course not. I love every subject.
Maria: Done!
Eric: What are you guys doing?
Maria: We just bought a birthday present for Jill.
Eric: Me too! Look guys! I got four tickets for the new musical *Dance City!* _____ (15) night.

Lessons 5-8: Grammar A

INTERESTS

Present simple: *do* and *does*

Do and does can be used to form *Yes/No* questions.	
Do I **Do** you + **main verb** **Do** we **Do** they	**Does** she **Does** he + **main verb** **Does** it
Do you **know** the band Coldplay? Yes, I **know** Coldplay. (shortened form) Yes, I **do**.	**Does** your roommate have a band? Yes, he **has** a band. (shortened form) Yes, he **does**.
Do you **like** snowboarding? No, I **don't like** snowboarding. (shortened form) No, I **don't**.	**Does** your girlfriend like snowboarding? No, she **doesn't like** snowboarding. (shortened form) No, she **doesn't**.

Part 1

Complete the questions with *Do* or *Does* and the correct form of the verb in parentheses.

1. A: _____Do_____ you and your roommate _____watch_____ reality shows? (watch)   B: Yes, we do.
2. A: _____ this music _____ like hip-hop? (sound)   B: No, it doesn't.
3. A: _____ Gong Li _____ a new movie out? (have)   B: Yes, she does.
4. A: _____ Lucas _____ to go to the movies? (like)   B: Yes, he does.
5. A: _____ your friends _____ sushi? (eat)   B: Yes, they do.

Part 2

Complete the answers with *do, don't, does,* or *doesn't.*

1. A: Do you like to watch comedies?   B: Yes, I _____ .
2. A: Does Marcus play the guitar?   B: No, he _____ .
3. A: Do Lisa and Bob like pizza?   B: Yes, they _____ .
4. A: Do you and your friends watch *The Amazing Chase*?   B: No, we _____ .
5. A: Does your band have a name?   B: Yes, we _____ !
6. A: Does Sara listen to jazz?   B: No, she _____ .
7. A: Does this concert end at midnight?   B: Yes, it _____ .
8. A: Do you want to eat at a restaurant tonight?   B: No, I _____ .

Lessons 5-8: Grammar B

INTERESTS

Compound nouns

A compound noun is a noun made up of two or more words. It acts as a single word.
skate + board → Is this your **skateboard**?
swimming + pool → Where's the **swimming pool**?
rock + climbing → My favorite sport is **rock climbing**.

A compound noun can be made up of nouns, verbs, adjectives, and prepositions.	
haircut →	noun + verb
toothpaste →	noun + noun
blackboard →	adjective + noun
skateboard →	verb + noun
mother-in-law →	noun + preposition + noun
swimming pool →	verb + noun

A compound noun can be
- open (space between words): tennis shoes, rock climbing
- hyphenated (hyphen between words): grown-ups, 18-year-olds
- closed (no space between words): breakfast, snowboarding

Part 1

Check the compound nouns in the sentences. (Use a dictionary to help you.)

1. Does the _____ big hotel have a __✓__ swimming pool?
2. It's a _____ long drive to the _____ skateboard park.
3. I have my _____ new boots, so let's go _____ rock climbing today.
4. Robbie and his _____ brother-in-law went _____ swimming today.
5. We went _____ skateboarding _____ last week.

Part 2

Complete the sentences with the correct form of a compound noun. (Use a dictionary to help you.)

1. A: Do you want to **climb** on the **rocks** today?   B: No, I don't like __rock climbing__.
2. A **board** for riding the **surf** is a _____.
3. If you **jump** with a **bungee**, you are _____.
4. When you **dive** from the **sky**, you are _____.
5. A: Do you like to ride a **bike** in the **mountains**?   B: No, I don't like _____.
6. A: Do you want to ride on a **raft** down the **river**?   B: Yes, I really enjoy _____.
7. A: What **shoes** do you wear when you play **tennis**?   B: I wear _____.

Lessons 5-8: Grammar C

INTERESTS

Prepositions in time expressions

Prepositions that show time include *at*, *in*, and *on*.		
at	a specific time	at 6:30
	night	at night
Class starts at 9 a.m. I like to watch movies at night.		
in	a specific month a specific year the morning the afternoon the evening	in February in 2009 in the morning in the afternoon in the evening
My birthday is **in** February. I lived in the U.S. **in** 2009. We eat breakfast **in** the morning.	They got married **in** the afternoon. We don't have class **in** the evening.	
on	a specific day of the week a specific date	on Monday on Dec. 30th
Vacation starts **on** Monday. The test is **on** September 15th.		

Part 1

Circle the correct preposition.

1. The concert starts on/**at** 8 p.m.
2. Is your birthday **on/in** December?
3. Lara's graduation party is **in/on** June 3rd.
4. The movie starts **at/on** 9 p.m. tonight.
5. We don't have snowboarding classes **in/at** night.
6. Mollie doesn't eat breakfast **in/at** the morning.

Part 2

Write the correct preposition: *at*, *in*, or *on*.

1. Do you eat dinner ___at___ 8:30 p.m.?
2. Milo visited Mexico _____ 2011.
3. The soccer game is _____ Saturday, April 26.
4. Kara likes to relax _____ the evening.
5. Nick was born _____ January 25, 1990.
6. I like to go for a walk _____ night.

Lesson 9: Vocabulary

PEOPLE

Part 1

A family tree shows all of the people in a family. Imagine this is part of your father's family tree. Write the words to finish the tree.

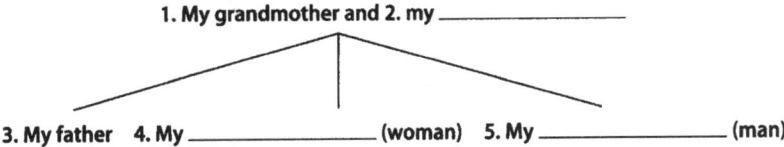

1. My grandmother and 2. my _____

3. My father   4. My _____ (woman)   5. My _____ (man)

Part 2

Look at the family tree in Part 1. Complete the sentences.

1. Person 1 and person 2 are my _____.
2. Person 4's daughter is my _____.
3. Person 5's son is my _____.
4. Person 5's son is my father's _____.
5. Person 4's daughter is my father's _____.
6. My mother and father are my _____.

Part 3

Complete the sentences with true information about you. In class, take turns reading your sentences with a partner.

1. I _____ two sisters.
2. My _____ is single.
3. My _____ is married.
4. My _____ is _____ years old.
5. I _____ an only child.
6. My _____ is older than me, but my _____ is younger than me.
7. I _____ children.
8. I _____ one brother.

Lesson 9: Reading & Writing

PEOPLE

Part 1

Read the e-mail below from Cynthia.

From: Cynthia Watson
Subject: Welcome to our home!
Date: May 5, 2013
To: Yumiko Matsuo

Dear Yumiko,

My name is Cynthia Watson, and you are going to stay with us for three months while you study English in the United States.

There are four people in our family. My husband James is a teacher. He loves kayaking. Do you want to try it while you are here? We have two children, my seven-year-old daughter Kelly, and my four-year-old son Kyle. Kelly loves to play outside with her cousin, Beka. She lives down the street with her parents, Frank and Sandy. They have a boat and want to take you for a ride in June. My parents, Austin and Nadine, live near us, too. They are going to have you over to swim in their pool during the summer.

We are so excited to meet you! See you next week!
Cynthia "Mom"

Complete the sentences.

1. Cynthia's niece's name is _____.
2. Nadine is Kyle's _____.
3. Beka's cousins are _____ and _____.
4. _____ is an only child.
5. Beka's uncle is _____, and her aunt is _____.

PAIR WORK Discuss the questions.

1. Would you like to stay with the Watson family? Give reasons for your answers.
2. What kind of interests would your perfect host family have?
3. Where would you like to go to study English? How long would you stay? Why?

Part 2

Write an e-mail to Cynthia to tell her about you and your family members. Finish by telling her you are also excited to meet her family.

Part 3

Share your e-mail with your partner. What are the most important things for schools to think about when they put host students with host families?

Lesson 10: Vocabulary

PEOPLE

Part 1

Are these personalities positive, negative, or both? In class, talk about your ideas with a partner.

| serious | shy | patient | smart | funny | quiet | friendly | confident |

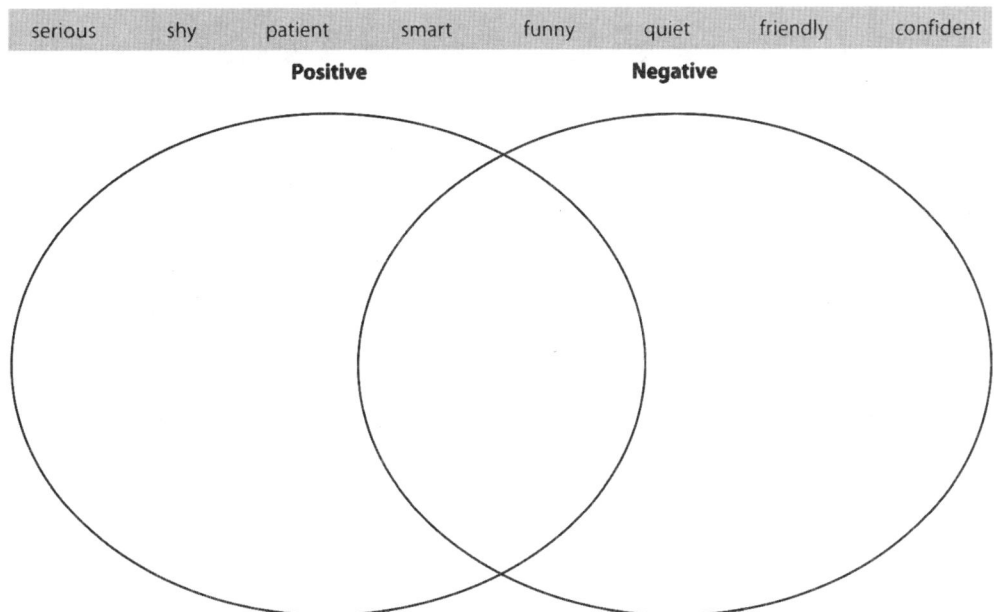

Part 2

Use the words from Part 1 to complete each sentence. You won't use one word.

1. You and your friend waited in a long line for 30 minutes. Your friend wasn't angry.
   She is _____.
2. While you waited in line, your friend talked to many people. She is also _____.
3. It was fun waiting with your friend, but you can't talk to other people very easily. You are kind of quiet and _____.
4. Your friend is good at studying English. He is very _____ and got an A on his last English test.
5. Your friend always thinks he will do well. People think he is _____.
6. Many people smile when your friend says interesting things. He is _____.
7. You always think a lot before you do things. You are _____.

Part 3

1. Think about you and your friend. Which sentences in Part 2 are true? _____
2. Which sentences aren't true? _____

Lesson 10: Reading & Writing

PEOPLE

Part 1

Read the e-mail from David.

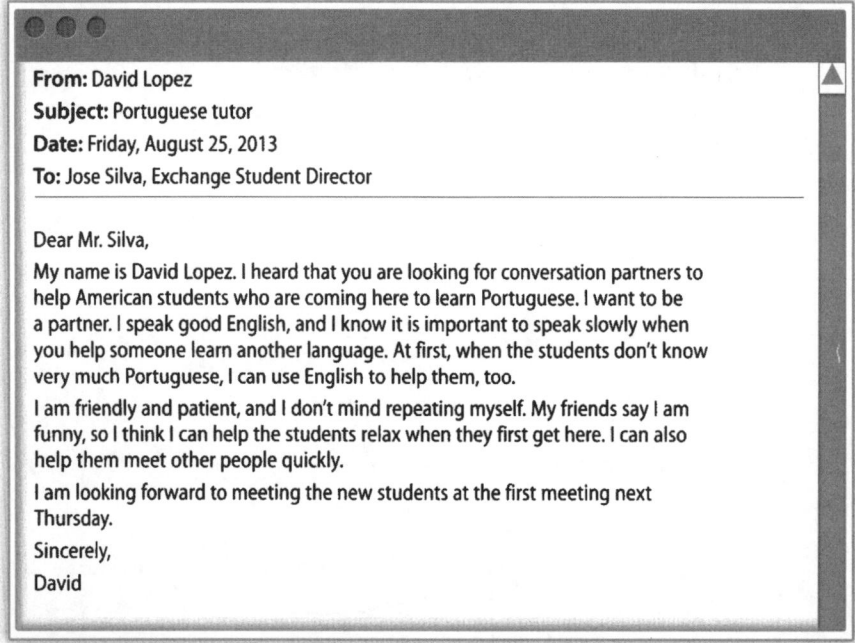

From: David Lopez
Subject: Portuguese tutor
Date: Friday, August 25, 2013
To: Jose Silva, Exchange Student Director

Dear Mr. Silva,

My name is David Lopez. I heard that you are looking for conversation partners to help American students who are coming here to learn Portuguese. I want to be a partner. I speak good English, and I know it is important to speak slowly when you help someone learn another language. At first, when the students don't know very much Portuguese, I can use English to help them, too.

I am friendly and patient, and I don't mind repeating myself. My friends say I am funny, so I think I can help the students relax when they first get here. I can also help them meet other people quickly.

I am looking forward to meeting the new students at the first meeting next Thursday.

Sincerely,
David

Complete the sentences.

1. David will help _____ learn a new language.
2. David speaks _____ and _____.
3. David and Mr. Silva _____ met before.
4. David _____ shy.
5. The first meeting is on _____, 2013.

PAIR WORK Discuss the questions.

1. Do you think David will be a good conversation partner? Give reasons for your answer.
2. What other types of personalities are good for conversation partners?
3. Should David correct all of the mistakes his partner makes? Why or why not?

Part 2

Imagine some Americans are visiting your school and you want to be a conversation partner. Write a short e-mail. Describe your personality and say why you will be a good partner.

Part 3

In class, compare your e-mails. What different types of personalities do your classmates have? Which is the best type to be a conversation partner?

Lesson 11: Vocabulary

PEOPLE

Part 1
Are these clothes tops (things you wear on the top part of your body), bottoms, or both? Write them in the correct place in the diagram.

jackets   jeans   shirts   T-shirts   shorts   skirts   sweaters   dresses   watches   bracelets   rings   belts

Tops   **Bottoms**

Part 2
Add three more kinds of clothes to the diagram in Part 1. In class, compare your ideas with a partner.

Part 3
Complete the sentences with words from Part 1. In class, talk about your ideas with a partner.

1. People wear _____ and _____ when it's cold.
2. People wear _____ and _____ when it's hot.
3. People wear _____ so they know what time it is.
4. People often wear _____ when they are married.
5. People often wear _____ to keep their jeans up.
6. Usually only women wear _____ and _____.

Lesson 11: Reading & Writing

PEOPLE

Part 1

Read the poster.

Clothing Forever
Where Fashion is Fun

Sale!   Sale!   Sale!
All summer clothes* on sale to make space for fall fashions!
Summer dresses 40% off
Save 10-60% on shirts and T-shirts
Summer skirts only $10 each
Hurry now. The sale ends Friday!
Be sure to stop by to see our new fall and winter clothes!
Boys' and girls' jeans and jean jackets
Women's jackets
Men's sweaters
Store hours: M-Th 10-9, F & Sat 10-10, Sun 10-5
7400 Galleria Drive
*No discount on designer clothes. Summer accessories not included in the sale. All sales final.

Mark the statements **T** (True) or **F** (False).

_____ 1. In the United States, you would probably see this poster in May.

_____ 2. Shorts are probably on sale, too.

_____ 3. This store only has clothing for children.

_____ 4. The store opens every day at 10 a.m.

_____ 5. A watch with summer flowers is also on sale.

 PAIR WORK Correct the false sentences with a partner.

Part 2

Think of your favorite store. Make a poster telling people about a sale at the store.

Part 3

Share your poster with a partner. Ask them what they want to buy and why. Write a list of the things you want from your partner's favorite store. What day is the best to go shopping there?

Lesson 12: Vocabulary

PEOPLE

Part 1

Find the 11 color words in the puzzle below. The words go

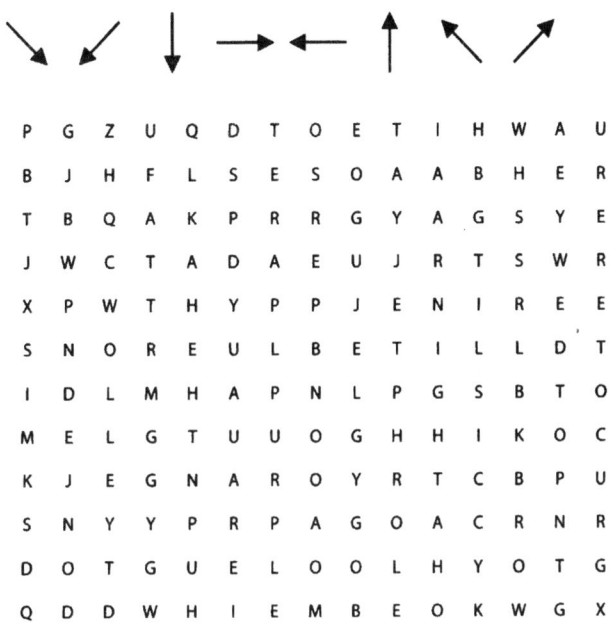

P	G	Z	U	Q	D	T	O	E	T	I	H	W	A	U
B	J	H	F	L	S	E	S	O	A	A	B	H	E	R
T	B	Q	A	K	P	R	R	G	Y	A	G	S	Y	E
J	W	C	T	A	D	A	E	U	J	R	T	S	W	R
X	P	W	T	H	Y	P	P	J	E	N	I	R	E	E
S	N	O	R	E	U	L	B	E	T	I	L	L	D	T
I	D	L	M	H	A	P	N	L	P	G	S	B	T	O
M	E	L	G	T	U	U	O	G	H	H	I	K	O	C
K	J	E	G	N	A	R	O	Y	R	T	C	B	P	U
S	N	Y	Y	P	R	P	A	G	O	A	C	R	N	R
D	O	T	G	U	E	L	O	O	L	H	Y	O	T	G
Q	D	D	W	H	I	E	M	B	E	O	K	W	G	X
F	A	N	L	A	S	L	E	Y	P	F	S	N	H	C
O	P	I	N	K	C	Z	D	P	Y	U	L	N	E	L

Part 2

Look at the letters you didn't circle. Write every 6th letter below to find the hidden message.

<u>T</u> <u>H</u> ___ ___ ___   ___ ___ ___

___ ___ ___ ___ ___   ___ ___ ___ ___ ___

___ ___ ___ ___   ___ ___   ___ ___ ___.

Part 3

Write sentences with three of the colors. In class, take turns reading them with a partner.

1. _____
2. _____
3. _____

Lesson 12: Reading & Writing

PEOPLE

Part 1

Read the page from the catalog below.

The Perfect Look

This jacket makes it easy to look great everywhere. Wear it with pants at the office, or for more informal situations, wear it with jeans. It comes in brown and black. $89.99

These shoes say, "I know who I am!" They feel great and have a unique look that will make people ask, "Where did you get those shoes?" $59

This shirt looks as good at 7 p.m. as it does at 7 a.m., so you can look your best all day long. In blue, green, pink, yellow, white, and black. $39.95

When you wear these jeans, all of your friends will say, "I love your jeans!" Perfect for day or night. $50

Circle the correct word to complete the sentence.

1. The shirt probably looks very good *unless/even after* you wear it many hours.
2. The shoes are *unusual/usual*.
3. The *shirt/jeans* comes in many colors.
4. You can wear the *shirt/jacket* in formal situations.
5. The shoes *can/cannot* talk.

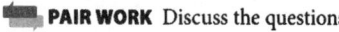 **PAIR WORK** Discuss the questions.

1. Do you want to wear the clothes in the catalog picture? Why or why not?
2. How often do you go shopping for clothes?
3. What is your favorite color? How often do you wear it?

Part 2

Choose three of your favorite pieces of clothing. What do you like about them? Write short descriptions like those you would find in a catalog.

Part 3

In class, read the descriptions you wrote, but don't say the type of clothing. Have your partner guess what kind of clothing you wrote about.

Lessons 9-12: Video Cloze

PEOPLE

Watch *Meet the Family* and fill in the blanks.

Tom: What time does your birthday party start tonight?

Jill: At 7:00. Maria is cleaning our apartment now.

Tom: No work for you on your birthday, huh?

Jill: That's right! That's a nice _____(1)_____!

Tom: Thanks! You look nice. Is that _____(2)_____ new?

Jill: Yes, I got it for tonight. Is it OK?

Tom: It's cool. I like it a lot.

Jill: Eric is here.

Eric: Hi, guys. Sorry I'm late. I wanted to get something new for your party tonight. What do you think?

Jill: It's an _____(3)_____ shirt.

Eric: So, we're going to get to meet your _____(4)_____.

Jill: Yes. They're arriving later this afternoon.

Eric: That's nice. But I'm always a little _____(5)_____ around new people.

Tom: Not me! Tell us about them!

Jill: Well, my _____(6)_____ is _____(7)_____. And shy. Dad doesn't say much at first.

Tom: And your _____(8)_____?

Jill: Mom is easy going and _____(9)_____, like me.

Tom: Do you have any _____(10)_____?

Jill: Yes, I have two _____(11)_____. As you can see, they love to play video games. Their names are Brent and David.

Tom: What is Brent _____(12)_____?

Jill: Brent is wearing the _____(13)_____ T-shirt. And David is wearing the gray _____(14)_____.

Jill: Brent will be there, but David doesn't live around here. He lives in Chicago. You can meet him another time.

Eric: How old are they?

Jill: Brent is 23 years old and David is 22. You'll also meet my _____(15)_____.

Eric: What's she like?

Jill: Grandma is great. She's 75 but she doesn't act or dress her age. Her style is very... different. But we love her!

Lessons 9-12: Grammar A

PEOPLE

This/That/These/Those

This/These refer to people or things that are near.
A: Who is this, Lisa?   B: **This** is my brother, Mark.
A: Whose shoes are you wearing?   B: **These** are my shoes.
That/Those refer to people or things that are not near.
A: Who was that person in the car?   B: **That** was my cousin.
B: How much are those shoes in the window?   B: **Those** shoes are $150.

	Singular	Plural
Near	this	these
Not near	that	those

Part 1

Circle the correct word.

1. **These**/**This** socks are purple.
2. **Those/That** T-shirt is nice. I'll take it, please.
3. Excuse me, how much are **those/that** pants?
4. **These/This** ring isn't new. It's my mother's.
5. **Those/That** shoes are black, not brown.
6. Where did you get **that/those** beautiful earrings?
7. I like to wear **this/these** sweater in the winter.

Part 2

Write the correct word: *this, that, these, those.*

1. A: I love your shirt. Where did you get it?   B: I got _____ shirt at The Shirt Shop.
2. Are _____ jeans over there blue or black?
3. A: I lost my earrings!   B: Wait! Here they are. Are _____ your earrings?
4. A: I like your hat. Is it new?   B: No, _____ hat is old.
5. A: You left a jacket at my house.   B: OK, I'll come over and get _____ jacket tonight.
6. The shoes in the closet are Dave's, but _____ shoes here are mine.
7. I have two jackets. _____ one is red, and the other one is black.

Lessons 9-12: Grammar B

PEOPLE

Adjectives and adverbs

Adjectives describe nouns or pronouns.	
a **red** shirt	my **older** sister
pretty shoes	a **funny** guy
Adjectives often follow a form of be (*am, is, are*). Adjectives come after the verb be and before the noun.	
I am **single**.	She is a **smart** student.
His jacket is **blue**.	My neighbors are **nice** people.
Adverbs can describe the action of a verb.	
You *speak* English **well**.	I **really** *like* your sweater.
I don't **usually** *wear* pink.	He **often** *wears* shorts.
Adverbs can be used to give information about adjectives.	
This TV show is **pretty** funny.	Your watch is **really** nice.
That dress is **incredibly** beautiful.	I'm **very** impatient.
Adverbs can be used to modify other adverbs. They come before the adverb they modify.	
She dresses **really** well.	You speak **very** confidently.

Part 1

Read the sentence. Decide if the word in bold is an adjective or an adverb. Circle your choice.

1. My older brother sings really **well**. — Adjective / (Adverb)
2. Jason's sister is a **pretty** good student. — Adjective / Adverb
3. Mara is a little **shy**, like me. — Adjective / Adverb
4. The Smith family **often** eats dinner together. — Adjective / Adverb
5. Your younger brother is incredibly **funny**! — Adjective / Adverb

Part 2

Write the adjective or adverb in parentheses in the correct place in the sentence.

1. My cousin is a ____*very*____ funny _____ guy. (very)
2. Oscar is wearing his _____ T-shirt _____ today. (favorite)
3. Dani speaks Spanish _____ pretty _____. (well)
4. Mike's friends _____ are _____. (creative)
5. Your grandparents are _____ nice _____! (incredibly)
6. Sam doesn't usually wear _____ shorts _____. (pink)

Lesson 13: Vocabulary

PEOPLE

Part 1

When do you usually do these activities? Write them in the correct place in the diagram.

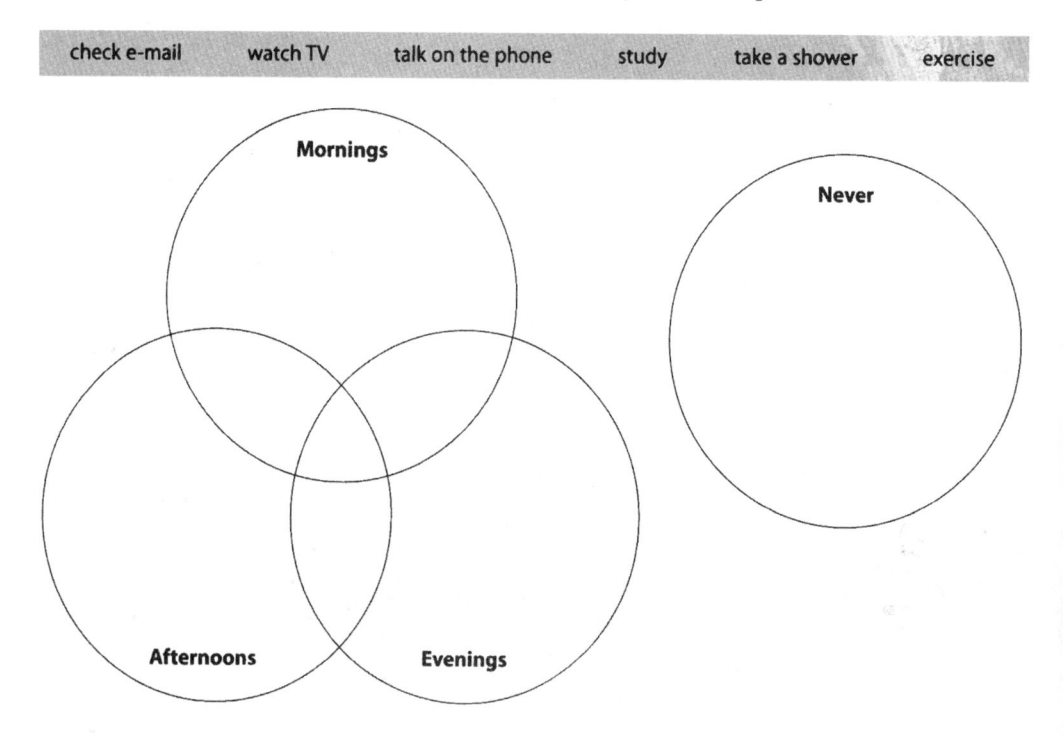

| check e-mail | watch TV | talk on the phone | study | take a shower | exercise |

(Venn diagram with three overlapping circles labeled **Mornings**, **Afternoons**, and **Evenings**, and a separate circle labeled **Never**.)

Part 2

Add three more activities to the diagram in Part 1. In class, compare your ideas with a partner.

Part 3

Answer the questions so they are true for you. In class, take turns asking and answering the questions with a partner.

1. On the days when you get up early, what time do you wake up? _____
2. When do you usually have lunch? _____
3. What time do you usually get home on Wednesdays? _____
4. What time do you usually eat dinner on Fridays? _____
5. When do you usually go to bed? _____
6. What time do you get to class on Thursday? _____
7. Do you usually talk on the phone every day? _____

Lesson 13: Reading & Writing

DAILY LIFE

Part 1

Read the journal article.

Mobile Phones before Bed

What do you usually do in the hour before you go to bed? If you are like most Americans 19-29 years old, you talk on your mobile phone, use your computer, or watch TV. But doing those things might be keeping you up at night.

These people said, on average, that they go to sleep at about midnight on weekdays and get up seven hours later. Interestingly, younger people, 13-18 years old, do the same things before bed, but they get up 40 minutes earlier on weekdays. However, because they also go to bed one hour earlier, they actually get more sleep than the older people.

Complete the sentences.

1. People who are 19-29 years old usually get up around _____.
2. This article is about people who live in _____.
3. The younger and older people _____ before bed.
4. People who are 13-18 years old go to bed at _____ and get up at _____ on weekdays.
5. People who are 13-18 years old sleep _____ than people who are 19-29 years old.

PAIR WORK Discuss the questions.

How would the students in your country answer the question in the article? How would you answer? What are the main reasons people stay up late instead of going to bed early?

Part 2

Write an article about the eating routines of young people in your country. What time and where do they eat? Who do they eat with? Imagine students in another country will read it.

Part 3

As a class, think about your **Pair work** answers and **Part 2** articles. Do sleep routines change eating routines?

Lesson 14: Vocabulary

DAILY LIFE

Part 1

Write one or two words to complete each activity. If a word is not needed, write an X.

1. _____ shopping
2. _____ work out
3. _____ the mall
4. _____ movies
5. _____ to eat
6. _____ to the library
7. _____ sports
8. _____ walk

Part 2

How often do you do the activities in Part 1? Put the activities in order from most often to least often. In class, talk about your ideas with a partner.

_____

_____

Part 3

Write the activities from Part 1 to complete the first sentence in each conversation. Write a follow-up question for the second person in each conversation. In class, practice the conversations with a partner.

1.
Lian: I love to _____.
Anna: _____?

2.
Eduardo: I _____ every day.
Keiko: _____?

3.
Maria: I usually _____ alone.
Manuel: _____?

4.
Andrew: I usually _____ with my friends.
Matteo: _____?

Lesson 14: Reading & Writing

DAILY LIFE

Part 1

Read the magazine article below.

Students Don't Study as Much as "Should"

A study of 472 university professors and 163,000 students has some people surprised. According to the study, the professors think their students should study at least 25 hours a week, but only 11 percent of the students said they study that much. 44 percent of the students study ten hours or less. About 35 percent of students who study less than ten hours a week get good grades.

Some students said that 25 hours a week is too much. That's 12.5 percent of each day! However, a professor said that it isn't just about reading. "Students have to remember details and think carefully about what they read." Some students, it seems, can do that more quickly than others.

Write the correct percentages next to each sentence.

11%   12.5%   about 35%   44%

1. _____ Students who study no more than ten hours a week.
2. _____ Students who study as much as the professors want.
3. _____ Percent of each day professors want students to study.
4. _____ Students who study less than ten hours a week but get good grades.

PAIR WORK Discuss the questions.
1. How many hours a week do you study?
2. How many hours a week do you think your teachers want you to study?
3. Do students who study some subjects have to study more than other students? Which subjects? Why?

Part 2

Think about your daily activities in the past. Write an e-mail to a friend. Talk about how your activities today are the same as or different than three years ago.

Part 3

With a partner, talk about your e-mail and how your activities will be the same or different three years from now.

Lesson 15: Vocabulary

DAILY LIFE

Part 1

When do you do these activities? Put the words into the best column for you. In class, talk about your ideas with a partner.

go out with friends feel my best	sleep in late stay up late	don't do much feel my worst	get up early
Saturday-Sunday	**Monday-Friday**	**Never**	
_____	_____	_____	
_____	_____	_____	
_____	_____	_____	
_____	_____	_____	
_____	_____	_____	

Part 2

Write each of the activities from Part 1 once to complete the story.

My name is Maria. During the week, I usually get up at 6:45, but yesterday I got up at 5:30. I don't usually (1) _____ like that. On Saturday night I usually (2) _____. We go out to eat or go to movies. I usually don't get home until after midnight. I don't really like to (3) _____ like that because the next day it's hard to get up. Because we stay out late, I usually (4) _____ on Sunday. Sometimes I get up at 11:00! When I do that, I (5) _____, and I especially don't study or work. I just watch TV and go shopping. My friends say, "I love Friday. I (6) _____ on Friday because the weekend is about to start." I (7) _____ on Sunday. I like to get up and go to bed at the same time every day.

Part 3

Answer the questions. In class, compare answers with a partner.

1. When you sleep in late, what time do you get up? _____
2. What time do you go to bed when you stay up late? _____
3. What do you do on days when you don't do much? _____
4. When you go out with friends, what do you usually do? _____
5. What do you do first after you get up? _____
6. What do you usually do after lunch? _____
7. What do you usually do after dinner? _____
8. What time do you usually have breakfast? _____
9. What do you do after that? _____

Lesson 15: Reading & Writing

DAILY LIFE

Part 1

Read the business e-mail below.

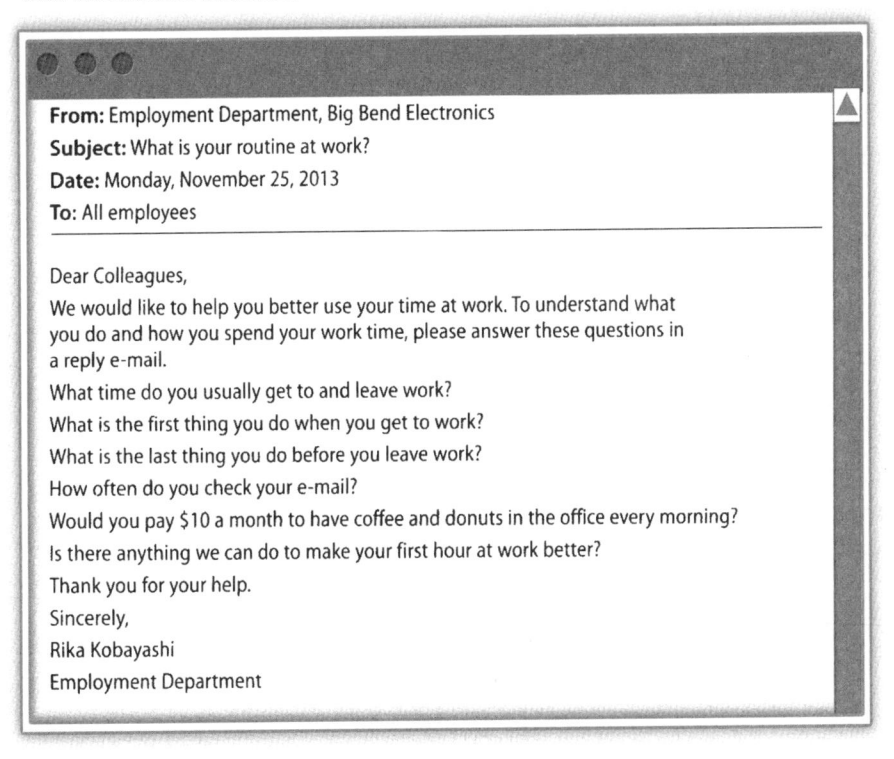

From: Employment Department, Big Bend Electronics
Subject: What is your routine at work?
Date: Monday, November 25, 2013
To: All employees

Dear Colleagues,
We would like to help you better use your time at work. To understand what you do and how you spend your work time, please answer these questions in a reply e-mail.
What time do you usually get to and leave work?
What is the first thing you do when you get to work?
What is the last thing you do before you leave work?
How often do you check your e-mail?
Would you pay $10 a month to have coffee and donuts in the office every morning?
Is there anything we can do to make your first hour at work better?
Thank you for your help.
Sincerely,
Rika Kobayashi
Employment Department

Answer the questions.

1. What does Rika ask the other employees to do? _____
2. Who is getting this e-mail? _____
3. What company does Rika work for? _____
4. Why are they sending this e-mail? _____
5. Which parts of the work day seem to be important to Rika? _____

PAIR WORK Discuss the questions.

Do you think most people are happy at their jobs? Talk about why it's important for employees to be happy and what companies can do to help them be happy.

Part 2

Send Rika an e-mail and answer her questions. (Change *work* to *school* if you don't have a job.)

Part 3

As a class, take turns saying your answers and find out which answers were the most popular.

Lesson 16: Vocabulary

DAILY LIFE

Part 1

Complete the sentences with class names.

1. Young children study 1+1=2 in _____ classes.
2. _____ is the study of how people think.
3. You study how to run companies when you study _____.
4. People who like to read sometimes study _____ in college.
5. _____ is the study of how groups of people act together.
6. People who like numbers and think about what they mean like _____.
7. If you know a lot about what happened 200 years ago, you know a lot about _____.
8. You have to know _____ to sell things.
9. _____ includes things related to money, including how to make, buy, and sell things.
10. Around the world, _____ is a popular language to study.

Part 2

Answer the questions. In class, compare your answers with a partner.

1. Which of the classes in Part 1 are you taking these days? _____
2. Which of those classes do you love? _____
3. Which do you not really like? _____

Part 3

What kind of people like taking the classes in Part 1? Choose seven more classes. Write the class and one or two characteristics for each person. In class, talk about your ideas with a partner.

English: like to talk with people from other countries
_____
_____
_____
_____
_____
_____
_____

Lesson 16: Reading & Writing

DAILY LIFE

Part 1

Read the e-mail below.

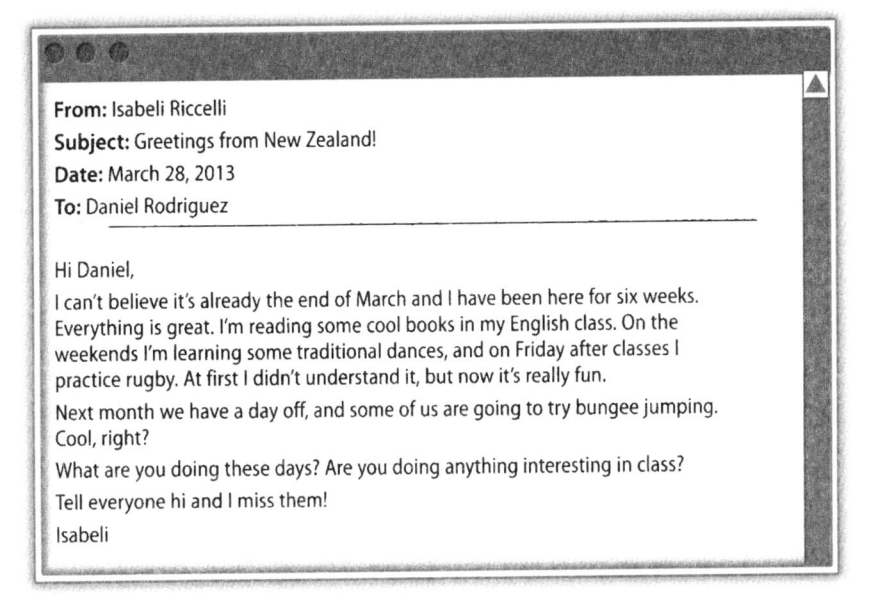

From: Isabeli Riccelli
Subject: Greetings from New Zealand!
Date: March 28, 2013
To: Daniel Rodriguez

Hi Daniel,

I can't believe it's already the end of March and I have been here for six weeks. Everything is great. I'm reading some cool books in my English class. On the weekends I'm learning some traditional dances, and on Friday after classes I practice rugby. At first I didn't understand it, but now it's really fun.

Next month we have a day off, and some of us are going to try bungee jumping. Cool, right?

What are you doing these days? Are you doing anything interesting in class?

Tell everyone hi and I miss them!

Isabeli

Mark the statements T (True) or F (False).

_____ 1. Daniel is in New Zealand now.

_____ 2. Daniel and Isabeli are probably classmates.

_____ 3. Isabeli went bungee jumping and thought it was cool.

_____ 4. Isabeli left her country in February.

_____ 5. Isabeli still doesn't understand rugby.

PAIR WORK Correct the false statements with your partner.

Part 2

Write an e-mail to Isabeli and answer her questions. Tell her something cool you have done this month.

Part 3

In class, share your answers to Isabeli. What is the interesting thing you've done in class? What is the cool thing you've done this month?

Lessons 13-16: Video Cloze

DAILY LIFE

Watch *Jill's Sunday* and fill in the blanks.

Jill: What are you doing, Eric?

Eric: Oh, I'm just _____(1)_____ for my history exam.

Jill: Your _____(2)_____ exam? That doesn't sound fun. You know, you look a little _____(3)_____. Are you OK?

Eric: Yeah, I'm just really busy right now.

Jill: Do you go to bed _____(4)_____?

Eric: I go to bed around 11:30.

Jill: What time do you _____(5)_____ _____(6)_____?

Eric: I usually get up at 7:00. But I have a lot of _____(7)_____ and I'm working on _____(8)_____ at that new supermarket. I'm trying to save money.

Jill: You need to go out and get some _____(9)_____. I exercise every day.

Eric: What kind of exercise do you do?

Jill: Just light exercise. Why don't you come out with me next _____(10)_____?

Eric: What do you do on Sundays?

Jill: Well, first I do some exercises at that really large park nearby. I get there at _____(11)_____. I exercise for about fifteen minutes. Then I run on a trail for about an hour. It's beautiful in the _____(12)_____.

Eric: I know what you mean. I like that park too!

Jill: Next, I eat a delicious breakfast.

Eric: I really enjoy _____(13)_____!

Jill: After that, I go for a swim nearby.

Eric: In the park?

Jill: No, there's a really great place to swim near the park.

Eric: That sounds nice.

Jill: After that I play volleyball. I play with the same team every Sunday. You can join us.

Eric: How long do you play?

Jill: About _____(14)_____ minutes. Later I eat a big _____(15)_____.

Eric: I love big lunches! How about I just meet you for lunch?

Lessons 13-16: Grammar A

DAILY LIFE

Information questions

In information questions with BE, the subject follows BE.		
Question Word	**BE**	**Subject**
Where	is	the gym?
When	is	the concert?
What time	is	the game?
How	are	you?

In information questions with DO, the subject comes between DO and the main verb.			
Question Word	**DO**	**Subject**	**Main verb**
Where	do	you	study?
When	does	the concert	start?
What time	does	class	end?
How	do	they	feel today?

Part 1

Use the words to write information questions with the correct form of BE.

1. where/the library   _Where is the library?_
2. what time/dinner today   _____?
3. when/the soccer game   _____?
4. how/your parents today   _____?
5. where/my English books   _____?
6. how/the weather in Miami today   _____?
7. what time/your dance lesson   _____?
8. where/the bus stop   _____?

Part 2

Use the words to write information questions with the correct form of DO.

1. when/you/wake up   _When do you wake up?_
2. what time/Karl/eat breakfast   _____?
3. where/Anna/work   _____?
4. how/Josh and Lisa/get to school everyday   _____?
5. when/we/have lunch today   _____?
6. what/Mike/do after class every day   _____?
7. what time/you/go to work today   _____?
8. what/you and your sister/do on Sundays   _____?

Lessons 13-16: Grammar B

DAILY LIFE

Present continuous

Use the simple present for habits, facts that are always true, or facts that are true for a long time.	
We usually **eat** lunch together in the cafeteria. (habit) Jill **has** two brothers. (a fact that is always true) We **live** in Miami. (a fact that is true for a long time)	
Use the present continuous (*be* + verb + *-ing*) for activities that are happening now, are true temporarily, or are going to happen in the near future.	
Happening now:	Someone **is knocking** on the door! Go see who it is! I'm **eating** lunch now. Can I call you back later?
True temporarily:	Alphonse **is working** at a restaurant these days. Theresa **is living** with her parents for the summer.
Going to happen in the near future:	You're **studying** in France next semester, right? I'm **getting** up early tomorrow.
Use the simple present for non-action verbs that are not usually used in the present continuous: believe, need, dislike, see, hate, smell, hear, taste, know, think (meaning "to believe"), like, understand, love, want	
I **love** my history class. Ben **hates** getting up early.	I **think** history is interesting. Dinner **smells** great!

Circle the correct verb to complete the sentence.

1. Julie **is eating/eats** lunch at noon every day.
2. Today, Julie and Fred **are having/have** lunch at 11:30 a.m.
3. Lisa **takes/is taking** a Spanish class next semester.
4. Alex **is sleeping/sleeps** late on Saturday mornings.
5. Tina **stays/is staying** home from school this week.
6. I **am going/go** to work early tomorrow morning.
7. Sara **studies/is studying** marketing this semester.
8. Mario **leaves/is leaving** for school at 8 a.m. every day.
9. Ryan **is understanding/understands** the math lesson.
10. I **love/am loving** living in Miami!
11. The twins **have/are having** two older brothers.
12. The Martins **are owning/own** a house in Chicago.
13. Henry **is hating/hates** to do homework right after school.
14. Chloe **is checking/checks** her e-mail almost every day.
15. My classmates **want/are wanting** to have a party at the end of the semester.

Lesson 17: Vocabulary

MY HOMETOWN

Part 1

Write the room that matches the definition.

1. _____ this room in homes often has a TV
2. _____ the room in homes where people eat
3. _____ the room in some houses where you wash your clothes
4. _____ the room in apartments where people usually sleep
5. _____ the place outside and near homes, often with grass, trees, and/or flowers
6. _____ the room in an apartment where you can take a shower
7. _____ the room in your apartment where you cook

Part 2

Which rooms in Part 1 do you have in your place?

_____

In class, compare answers with a partner.

Part 3

How much time do you spend in the rooms in Part 2? Put them in order from the most time to the least time.

_____

_____

Part 4

Use the words below to write about your place or your English classroom. In class, takes turns reading your sentences with a partner.

| big | comfortable | convenient | noisy | quiet | small |

_____

_____

_____

_____

_____

Lesson 17: Reading & Writing

MY HOMETOWN

Part 1

Read the advertisement for an apartment.

Vista Bay at the Commons

Vista Bay at the Commons is the newest group of apartments in the southwest part of the city. It's just minutes from the train station and also near shopping and the best schools. Even though it's convenient, it's also quiet. No more sleepless nights because of noisy cars! You won't hear anything in our wonderful bedrooms.

You'll enter your new home through the living room, and once inside, you'll forget about everything else! You can relax as you cook in the huge, sunny kitchen or talk with friends in the cute dining room. Everyone will love the views out the windows of the living room, and you'll love the convenience of a laundry room, which is right next to the bathroom. No more taking your dirty clothes down the street to get them cleaned.

Call today to see these new apartments before they are gone. 800-741-9635.

Circle the correct word to complete each sentence.

1. The *dining room/kitchen* is big.
2. You probably don't see a *wall/park* through the living room windows.
3. The apartment has *five/six* rooms.
4. The writer wants us to think Vista Bay is *louder/quieter* than many other apartments.
5. In the last line of this ad, "they are gone" means the apartments will be *rented/moved*.

PAIR WORK Discuss the questions.

1. What important information is missing from the advertisement?
2. In your country, how many people would probably live in this apartment? Why?
3. Do you think you would you like to live in this apartment? Why?

Part 2

Write an advertisement about the perfect apartment. Describe it and include the good things about it.

Part 3

Share your advertisement with a partner. Does he/she agree that it is the perfect apartment? Compare your advertisements. How similar or different are they?

Lesson 18: Vocabulary

MY HOMETOWN

Read the hints and write the words to complete the crossword puzzle.

Across
3. It keeps food cold in the summer.
4. It washes the dishes.
5. You open the door and put things in it.
6. You sit on them.
8. You sleep on it.
9. You put clothes in it.
10. You cook on it.
12. Two or three people can sit on it in the living room.

Down
1. They help you see at night.
2. A short table, usually in the living room.
7. You put things on them. They're on walls.
11. You can watch the news on it.

Lesson 18: Reading & Writing

MY HOMETOWN

Part 1

Read the page from a brochure.

Students' Suggestions

We know you have a lot of things to buy for your new life here at the school. On this page, we've included students' ideas about the best places to buy them.

Coffee tables, Dressers

Why don't you buy them used? They are much cheaper than new ones, and they usually still look good. New Homes is the best place to buy them, and they will bring the furniture to your apartment for free.

TVs

This is one thing you should buy new. You'll use it a lot, and you don't know how long used ones will last. The Best TVs on Orchard Road has the most choices, and their prices are pretty good.

Beds, Sofas

Almost every student we talked to said Sleep World is the only place to get beds and sofas, but a few students said World of Sleep isn't bad.

Good luck shopping!

Answer the questions.

1. Who is this article for? _____
2. What should they buy new? _____
3. Is there only one place that sells beds and sofas? _____
4. Where is the TV store that students suggested? _____
5. Why do students suggest New Homes? _____

PAIR WORK Discuss the questions.

1. In your country, what things are usually in apartments that you rent?
2. In your country, where do students usually live during university?
3. Look at the suggestions in the article. What things do you have to have in an apartment? What things could you live without?

Part 2

Imagine a new student is moving to your area. List one or more good places for them to buy used or new furniture for an apartment.

Part 3

In class, agree on the best places to buy used and new furniture in the area. Do you prefer new or used furniture? Why?

Lesson 19: Vocabulary

MY HOMETOWN

Part 1

Match the places on the left with their definitions on the right.

1. bank
2. drugstore
3. hair salon
4. movie theater
5. department store
6. mall
7. library
8. post office

A. a place where you can buy many different things
B. a place where you go to watch films
C. a big building with many small stores inside
D. a place where you get and keep your money
E. a place where you buy things to help you when you are sick
F. a place where you can send a letter
G. a place women go to get their hair cut
H. a place where you can read books and magazines

Part 2

Complete the sentences with information that is true for you. In class, take turns reading your sentences with a partner.

1. _____ is the best movie theater for seeing movies.
2. A department store _____ the best place to shop for clothes.
3. The nearest library is _____.
4. At the mall, I like to hang out with friends at _____.
5. There is a good hair salon _____.
6. The _____ is near the bank.
7. Many people go to _____
   because it's the _____ drugstore.
8. The nearest post office is _____.

Lesson 19: Reading & Writing

MY HOMETOWN

Part 1

Read the notice below.

Lost cat
$$$ REWARD $$$

Have you seen this cat?

Her name is Kitty. She is friendly and loves people.
I lost her on Friday, March 7, between 7:20 p.m. and 7:50 p.m. We were near the post office on King Street. It's across from the City Park, the one with the City Library. I saw Kitty going toward the bus stop that is next to the supermarket on Third Avenue. My apartment is near Forty-Third Avenue, so I don't think she will walk home.
Maybe you thought she didn't have a family so you took her home, but I miss her.
Please call with any information. Sally 555-028-7469.

Mark the statements **T** (True) or **F** (False).

_____ 1. Kitty lost Sally.

_____ 2. The bus stop is near Second Avenue.

_____ 3. The City Library is in the City Park.

_____ 4. The supermarket is on Forty-Third Avenue.

_____ 5. Sally's apartment is too far for Kitty to walk.

_____ 6. Sally lives near King Street.

PAIR WORK Correct the false statements with your partner. Then talk about what else she could do to try to find her cat.

Part 2

Imagine you found Kitty. Write Sally an e-mail. In it, decide when and where you will meet to give the cat back. How much of a reward do you want from Sally?

Part 3

A reward is money you get for doing something good. Are rewards popular in your country? In class, talk about how much reward you would want to return Sally's cat. Also talk about how much reward you would give if you lost something important.

Lesson 20: Vocabulary

MY HOMETOWN

Read the conversations. What place are they talking about? Write your answer on the line. In class, practice the conversations with a partner.

1. _____

A: Hi. Do you want to go to a baseball game on Sunday?
B: Sounds great!

2. _____

Mom: It's a beautiful day. Why don't you go out to play?
Son: There's a soccer game on the field, and I'm too old for the other things there.

3. _____

Driver: Where to?
A: The Carlton Hotel, please.

4. _____

A: Excuse me. Does this one go to Pennsylvania Avenue?
B: No, but the next bus does. It's number 17A.

5. _____

Announcement: Next stop, Diamond Hill. Change here for the East Kowloon Line.

6. _____

Radio announcer: The cars on I-105 aren't moving at all. You should take another road unless you like sitting in your car and listening to the radio for a long time!

7. _____

A: Do you want to go fishing at 2:00?
B: Sure. I'll meet you there.

8. _____

News reporter: Last night, some trees fell over it, so cars on Highway 26 can't cross the river this morning.

Lesson 20: Reading & Writing

MY HOMETOWN

Part 1

Read the text messages.

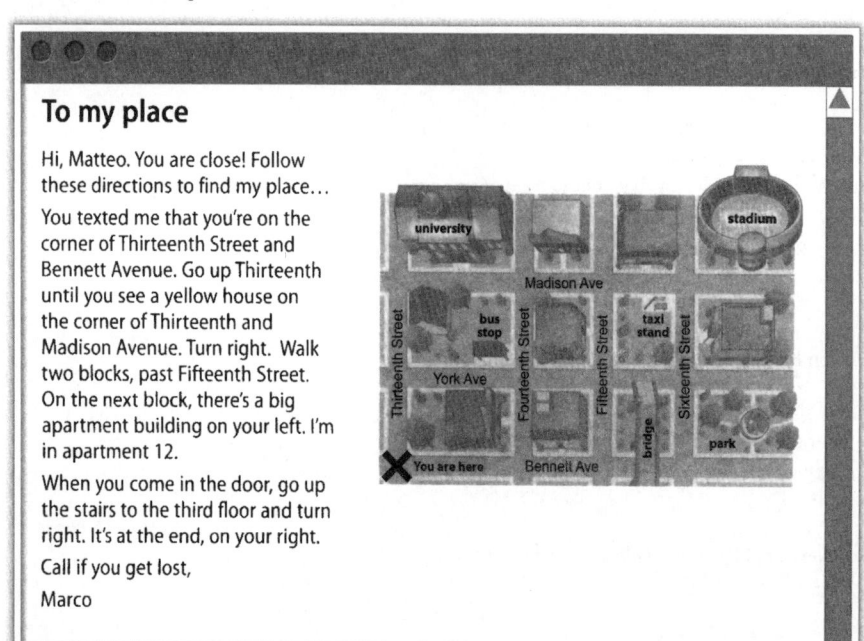

To my place

Hi, Matteo. You are close! Follow these directions to find my place...

You texted me that you're on the corner of Thirteenth Street and Bennett Avenue. Go up Thirteenth until you see a yellow house on the corner of Thirteenth and Madison Avenue. Turn right. Walk two blocks, past Fifteenth Street. On the next block, there's a big apartment building on your left. I'm in apartment 12.

When you come in the door, go up the stairs to the third floor and turn right. It's at the end, on your right.

Call if you get lost,

Marco

Answer the questions.

1. Who is giving directions? _____
2. Does Matteo have to go under a bridge to get to the apartment? _____
3. What street is Matteo on when he sends the text? _____
4. What happened before Marco wrote the text? _____
5. From Thirteenth Street, how many blocks is it to the apartment? _____

PAIR WORK Using the map, practice giving directions. Use other ways to get to Marco's house.

Part 2

Write a short text to your mom. Explain how to get from your school to your favorite café or restaurant.

Part 3

In class, compare the directions you wrote. Does your partner understand them? Could they meet you at your favorite café or restaurant using your directions?

Lessons 17-20: Video Cloze

MY HOMETOWN

Watch *Maria Goes Shopping* and fill in the blanks.

Tom: So, how do you and Jill like your _____(1)_____?

Maria: Oh, it's great. It's a little _____(2)_____, but it's really convenient and _____(3)_____.

Tom: Yeah, this is a good _____(4)_____. Eric and I like living here.

Maria: By the way, where do you buy your groceries?

Tom: We usually go to Larson's. It's on the _____(5)_____ of Pine Street and First Avenue.

Maria: It's near the _____(6)_____, right?

Tom: Yep.

Maria: Jill and I usually go to Market Fair.

Tom: Is it by the park?

Maria: Right. It's not far at all. We walk there.

Tom: Maybe I'll go there next time. So do you have everything you need for your apartment now?

Maria: I'm sleeping on the _____(7)_____ at the moment. Do you know where I could get a _____(8)_____? Also, I want to get some chairs and a bookcase.

Tom: Do you need a _____(9)_____? I have one I'm not using.

Maria: No, I have a desk, but thank you.

Tom: You know, why don't you check out the _____(10)_____? They have everything you need, and their stuff is really cheap.

Maria: The Superstore! I think I saw an ad for them on TV. Is it near?

Tom: It's on Mason Street. You know, just after the movie theater. It's _____(11)_____ from Pace _____(12)_____.

Maria: Do they have parking?

Tom: The parking lot is around the corner on West Avenue. Go _____(13)_____ the store, take a right, and you come to the parking lot.

Maria: Great. I'll stop by today. Say, want to come with me?

Tom: I do need a new lamp, but I can't go today. I have to study.

Maria: I'll pick it up for you.

Tom: Are you sure?

Maria: Why not? What kind of _____(14)_____ do you want?

Tom: I just need a lamp that works. My _____(15)_____ is too dark.

Maria: OK, I think I know just what you need to brighten your room.

Tom: Come in!

Maria: I found the perfect lamp for your room! Isn't it bright?

Tom: It definitely is. Thanks, Maria.

Lessons 17-20: Grammar A

MY HOMETOWN

Prepositions of location

Prepositions of location explain where something is.		
We usually use **at** for a point Let's eat **at** my place. **in** for an enclosed space I live **in** Chicago. **on** for a surface My apartment is **on** Green Street		
at the door	**in** Athens	**on** the floor
at the entrance	**in** the drawer	**on** the table
at my place	**in** the building	**on** the desk
at the mall	**in** the living room	**on** the page
at the store	**in** a car	**on** the board
at the bus stop	**in** the yard	**on** Oak Street

Part 1

Circle the correct preposition to complete the sentence.

1. Evan lives **at/in/on** Chicago.
2. Rachel's apartment is **at/in/on** Fourth Street.
3. The laundry room is **at/in/on** the 3rd floor of my building.
4. I'll meet you **at/in/on** the entrance to the mall at 10 a.m.
5. There are some pretty trees **at/in/on** the yard.
6. Allison put a lamp **at/in/on** the desk.
7. Let's have dinner **at/in/on** my place this weekend.
8. I keep my keys **at/in/on** the desk drawer.

Part 2

Complete the sentences with *at*, *in*, or *on*.

1. Jason lives ____on____ the 5th floor of my apartment building
2. The bookshelves are _____ the living room.
3. I get the bus _____ this bus stop every morning.
4. How many bedrooms are there _____ the apartment?
5. Eric bought a TV _____ Electric City.
6. There's a movie theater _____ Green Street.
7. I hear a knock. I think someone's _____ the door.
8. Is there a laundry room _____ the building?

Lessons 17-20: Grammar B

MY HOMETOWN

There is/There are

Use *there is/there are* to talk about the presence or existence of things in a place.		
Affirmative		
There	is	a school on the corner.
	are	three bedrooms in my apartment.
*Note: The contraction for *there is* is *there's*. There's a park across the street from my house.		There is **no** contraction for *there are*.
Negative		
There	isn't	a lamp in the living room.
	is no	mall in my town.
	aren't	any good supermarkets near here.
	are no	chairs at this table.
Yes/No Questions		
Is	there	a good place to buy furniture around here?
Are		any good restaurants near here?
Short Answers		
Yes, *there is*. Yes, *there are*.		No, *there isn't*. No, *there aren't*.

Part 1

Circle the correct form of *there is/there are*.

1. **(There's)/There are** a new sofa in the living room.
2. **Is there/Are there** a dining room in your new apartment?
3. **There is no/There aren't any** bus stops near my place.
4. **Is there/Are there** any trees in the yard?
5. **There's/There are** a small bedroom next to the living room.

Part 2

Complete the conversations with the correct form of *there is/there are*.

1. A: _____**Is there**_____ a library near here? B: No, _____**there isn't**_____.
2. A: _____ any nice parks in your hometown? B: Yes, _____.
3. A: _____ a Chinese restaurant on your street? B: Yes, _____.
4. A: _____ any chairs in the dining room? B: Yes, _____.
5. A: _____ a lamp in the bedroom? B: No, _____.
6. A: _____ any furniture stores at the mall? B: No, _____.

Lessons 17-20: Grammar C

MY HOMETOWN

Where can I...?

Use Where can I...? with a verb to ask about locations.			
Where	**can**	**Subject**	**Main Verb**
Where	can	I	get a new cell phone?
Where	can	we	find a used sofa?
Where	can	I	buy a new lamp?

Part 1

Unscramble the sentences.

1. buy a TV/can/I/where   Where can I buy a TV?
2. can/find some chairs/we/where _____?
3. I/buy a refrigerator/can/where _____?
4. where/I/get some bookshelves/can _____?
5. see some modern art/we/can/where _____?
6. where/I/can/buy some cool used clothes _____?

Part 2

Write the questions. Use *Where can I...?* with the verb in parentheses.

1. I need a used lamp. (get) _____.
2. I like foreign movies. (see) _____.
3. We want some Chinese food. (eat) _____.
4. I want some comic books. (buy) _____.
5. I like live music. (hear) _____.
6. We need cheap furniture. (get) _____.
7. I want a used sofa. (find) _____.
8. I need a dresser. (buy) _____.
9. We need stuff for the kitchen. (get) _____.

Lessons 17-20: Grammar D

MY HOMETOWN

What is...like?

> **What is...like?** means "Describe somebody or something. Tell me about it or them."
> Use the verb **is**. **Like** is used as a preposition.
>
> A: **What is** your new friend **like**?
> B: She's really nice. She's funny and smart.
> A: **What is** your apartment **like**?
> B: It's small, but convenient.
>
> **We don't use like in the answer.**
>
> A: What is your new friend like?
> B: She's ~~like~~ really nice.
>
> **The use of like with does or do means preference. In this case, like is used as a verb.**
>
> A: What **does** your new friend **like**? (What does your new friend prefer?)
> B: She likes rock music. She also likes to dance.
>
> **How asks about health. It doesn't ask for a description.**
>
> A: **How** is your new friend?
> B: She's doing well. She'll get out of the hospital next week.

Part 1

Match the questions and the answers.

__f__ 1. What is Jessica like?   a. She's not well. She has a cold.
____ 2. What does Jessica like?   b. I'm fine. Thanks for asking.
____ 3. How is Jessica?   c. She likes pizza and sushi.
____ 4. What is your English class like?   d. It's small, but it has a nice yard.
____ 5. How are you today?   e. It's fun and interesting.
____ 6. What is your new apartment like?   f. She's really nice.

Part 2

Write answers about you.

1. A: What is your English class like?   B: __It's easy. We don't have a lot of homework__.
2. A: What is your teacher like?   B: _____.
3. A: What do you like?   B: _____.
4. A: What does your friend like?   B: _____.
5. A: How is your friend today?   B: _____.
6. A: What is your friend like   B: _____.
7. A: What is your place like?   B: _____.

Lesson 21: Vocabulary

SHOPPING

Part 1

Rank these things from 1 (the most expensive) to 6 (the least expensive).

_____ a haircut   _____ bus fare

_____ a cup of coffee   _____ a taxi ride across town

_____ a movie ticket   _____ museum admission fee

Part 2

Use your ideas from Part 1 to complete the conversations. You can use some things more than once. In class, practice the conversations with a partner.

1.

A: Museum admission fees are _____ than movie tickets.

B: I know. _____ are too expensive for me.

2.

A: I think _____ is reasonable.

B: Me, too. But it also depends on the place. At _____, _____ costs _____, but at _____ it costs _____.

3.

A: _____ can cost _____!

B: Yeah, but the cost depends on where you go.

4.

A: I think _____ costs the least, and _____ costs the most.

B: I think it depends. _____ is usually more expensive than _____, but sometimes _____ is even more expensive!

Part 3

How often do you pay for the things in Part 1? Write them in order from the most often to the least often (never). In class, talk about your ideas with a partner.

_____

_____

_____

_____

_____

Lesson 21: Reading & Writing

SHOPPING

Part 1

Read the e-mail below from Marina.

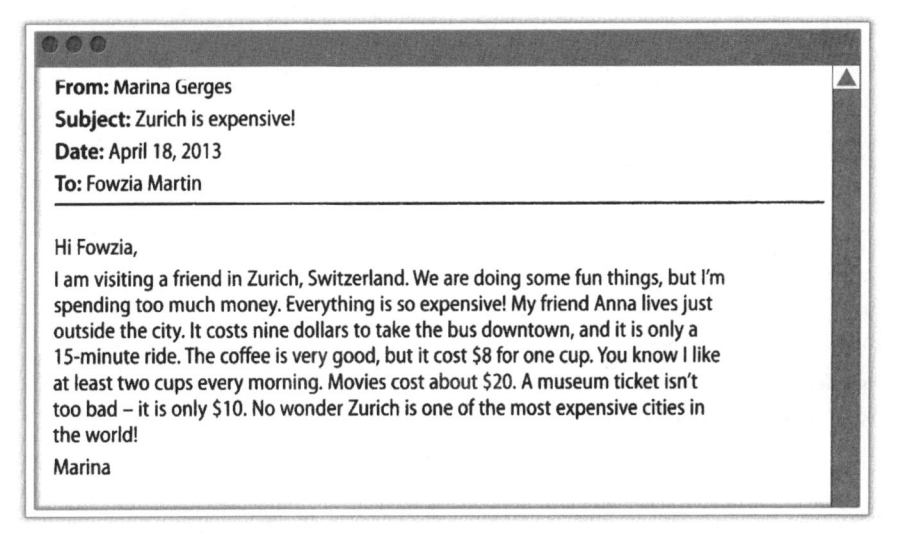

From: Marina Gerges
Subject: Zurich is expensive!
Date: April 18, 2013
To: Fowzia Martin

Hi Fowzia,
I am visiting a friend in Zurich, Switzerland. We are doing some fun things, but I'm spending too much money. Everything is so expensive! My friend Anna lives just outside the city. It costs nine dollars to take the bus downtown, and it is only a 15-minute ride. The coffee is very good, but it cost $8 for one cup. You know I like at least two cups every morning. Movies cost about $20. A museum ticket isn't too bad – it is only $10. No wonder Zurich is one of the most expensive cities in the world!
Marina

Write the correct price next to each item.

1. bus fare _____ $8
2. a cup of coffee _____ $9
3. a movie ticket _____ $10
4. museum admission _____ $20

PAIR WORK Discuss the questions.

1. Do you think Marina is having a good or a bad visit? Why?
2. What prices are important to visitors and tourists? Which are more important for people who live in a city?

Part 2

Write an e-mail to a friend about a city you know. What are the prices like? What do different things cost?

Part 3

Share your e-mail with a partner. Did you write about the same city? What prices were the same/different?

Lesson 22: Vocabulary

SHOPPING

Part 1

For each thing, write three examples.

1. clothes   <u>pants, shorts, a sweater</u>
2. makeup _____
3. toys _____
4. sports equipment _____
5. electronics _____
6. furniture _____
7. CDs _____
8. video games _____

In class, compare answers with a partner.

A: Pants, shorts, and a sweater are examples of clothes.
B: Yeah. And so are jeans, a jacket, and a T-shirt.

Part 2

What do you think about each of the things in Part 1? Put them in the diagram. In class, with your partner talk about why you put each one where you did.

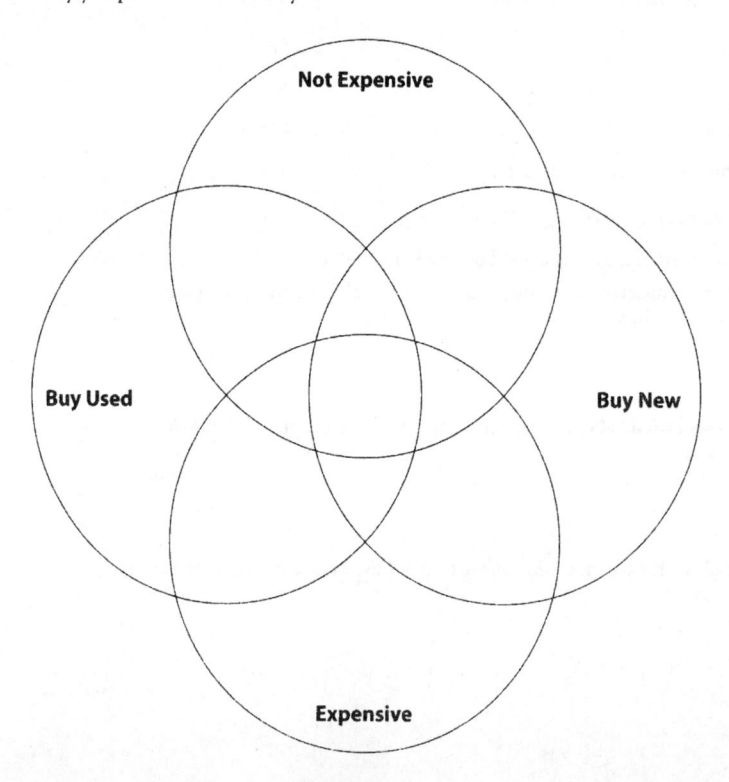

Not Expensive

Buy Used

Buy New

Expensive

62

Lesson 22: Reading & Writing

SHOPPING

Part 1

Read the article below about bargaining in Mexico.

Bargaining tips

You can find great bargains in Mexico if you know what you are doing. Most people bargain in markets. Follow the tips below and save money.

- Go early in the morning. You can get a better price.
- Bring your money in small bills and change.
- Be friendly. Say nice things about the items. Smile and ask questions.
- Know the prices ahead of time. You shouldn't start off with too low a price.
- Pick the item up and look at it. Show you are interested, but not too interested. The owner will say a price. You can offer a lower price.
- Don't get mad. If you don't like the price, walk away. You can look around and come back later.

Complete the sentences.

1. Most people bargain in _____ in Mexico.
2. You can get a lower price sometimes if you go _____.
3. It is good to know the _____ of things before you go.
4. You can _____ something up to show you are interested.
5. You can _____ if you don't like the price.

PAIR WORK Discuss the questions.

1. Why should you be friendly?
2. What are some ways to show you are interested?
3. What do you think the seller will do if you walk away?

Part 2

Write tips for bargaining in your country or a country you know well. When do people go? How do they bargain? How do they show they are interested? What can people bargain for?

Part 3

Share your tips with a partner. Do you have any different tips?

Lesson 23: Vocabulary

SHOPPING

Part 1

How do you buy these things? Put them in the diagram. In class, with your partner talk about why you put each one where you did.

newspapers   energy drinks   magazines   vitamins   candy   flowers   phone cards   gum

Online   In Stores   Never Buy

Part 2

Answer the questions, giving reasons when you can. In class, take turns asking and answering the questions with a partner.

1. How often do you shop for clothes?

2. When do you get flowers?

3. What kind of magazines do you read?

4. When do you buy used comic books?

5. How often do you buy gum?

6. Do you ever use a phone card?

7. How often do you read newspapers on the Internet?

8. Do you often buy candy?

Lesson 23: Reading & Writing

SHOPPING

Part 1

Read the article below.

Media Habits in Americans between 8 and 18

American children and teenagers spend almost 11 hours every day on media. They usually do more than one thing at a time. For example, they listen to music and work on their computers. They read a book for school while they are watching TV. American kids watch TV about 4.5 hours every day. For most families, the TV is usually on during meals.

Something is always on. Children and teenagers listen to music 2.5 hours every day. They use computers about 1.5 hours each day. They only read books, newspapers, and magazines about 4 hours each week. In fact, most young people almost never read newspapers or magazines. If they need news, they read it online. Young people don't read often just because they don't like it. In fact, 20% said they never read for fun.

Mark the statements **T** (True) or **F** (False).

_____ 1. Young people in the United States watch TV often.

_____ 2. Families often watch TV during dinner.

_____ 3. Children and teenagers usually do one thing at a time.

_____ 4. They listen to music about 1.5 hours a day.

_____ 5. They also read newspapers and magazines often.

_____ 6. Young people read more than they watch TV.

PAIR WORK Discuss the questions.

1. How often do you watch TV?
2. How often do you read? What is your favorite thing to read (books, websites, magazines)?
3. Are young people in your country different from Americans? How?

Part 2

Write sentences about your own media use. Use expressions of frequency. Say something about each:

- TV use
- computer use
- listening to music
- the different things you read

Part 3

Share your sentences with a classmate. What is similar? What is different?

Lesson 24: Vocabulary

SHOPPING

Part 1

Which word is different? Circle it. In class, with a partner talk about why it is different.

1. heavy — (thick) — light
2. fast — slow — thin
3. quiet — cheap — expensive
4. noisy — quiet — wide
5. dark — narrow — wide
6. thin — thick — bright
7. small — noisy — large
8. dark — narrow — bright

Part 2

What can you describe with the words in Part 1? Put them in the diagram. In class, with your partner talk about why you put each one where you did.

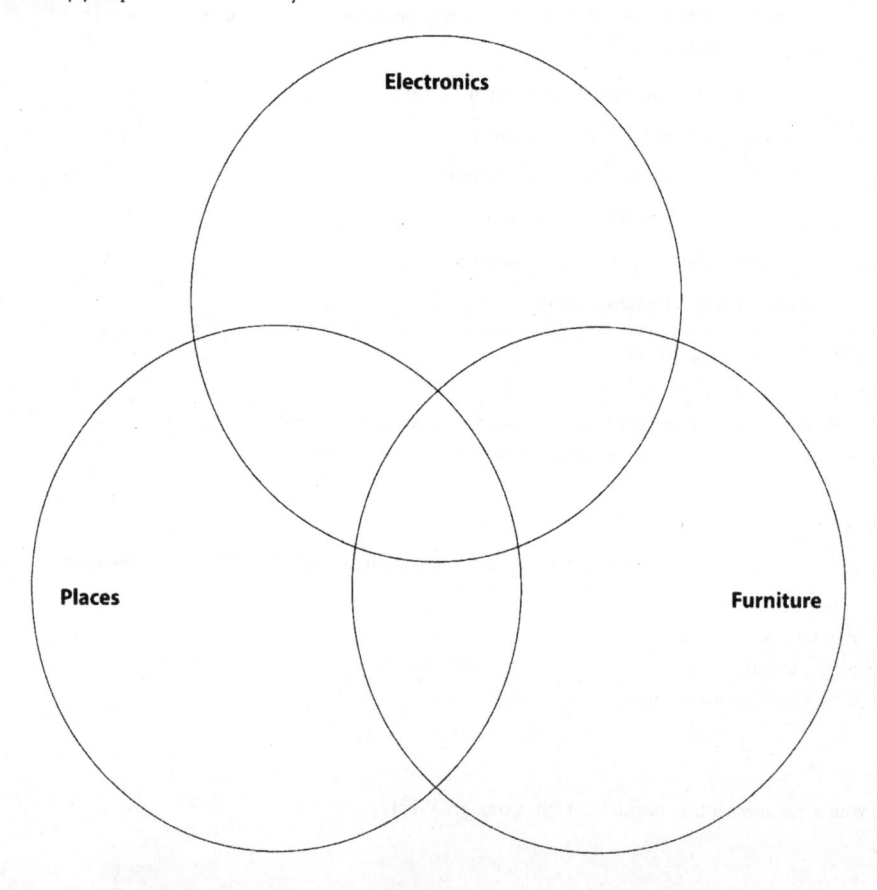

- Electronics
- Places
- Furniture

Lesson 24: Reading & Writing

SHOPPING

Part 1

Read the review from a student newspaper.

Your City Beat
New Art Museum a Must-See

The Adams Modern Art Museum opens this weekend. Don't miss it. The building has a cool design with an open lobby. There are many windows so all the rooms are light. Most of the paintings are bright and colorful. The garden outside blocks the noisy city streets. It is very quiet in the museum. You can walk around and look at the paintings. Or, you can drink a cup of coffee in the garden café. This weekend, they will have music from 7 p.m. to 9 p.m. on Friday night and again from 2 p.m. to 4 p.m. on Saturday afternoon. Admission is not expensive – only $5 – but this weekend it is free!

Circle the correct word to complete the sentence.

1. The museum's lobby is *narrow/wide*.
2. The rooms in the museum are *dark/light*.
3. The streets outside the museum are *quiet/noisy*.
4. You can *look at paintings/drink coffee* in the garden.
5. Admission to the museum is usually *cheap/expensive*.

PAIR WORK Discuss the questions.

1. Would you like to go to this museum? Why or why not?
2. What places do you like to go to in your city? Why?
3. The article is a review. The writer says if something is good or bad and gives reasons. Does this writer like the museum?
4. What kinds of things do people write reviews about?

Part 2

Look at the things below. Choose one and write a review. Talk about its qualities.

a car   a tablet   a place in your city   your own idea

Part 3

Post your review on a wall in the classroom. Walk around and read the reviews by your classmates. Which thing(s) do you want to see/use/visit?

Lessons 21-24: Video Cloze

SHOPPING

Watch *Eric's Lucky Chair* and fill in the blanks.

Tom: Your phone has a really cool design.

Jill: I really like it. It's light and thin. I can even video chat with my friends! I also buy tons of apps.

Tom: How _____(1)_____ do you buy apps?

Jill: I buy them every day.

Tom: Wow! That's a lot of money.

Jill: No, sometimes they're _____(2)_____.

Tom: I need a new phone.

Jill: What's yours like? Wow. That is really big.

Tom: Yes, but I can hear the other person really well.

Eric: Hi, guys!

Jill: What are you doing, Eric?

Eric: Oh. I'm going to _____(3)_____ this chair online.

Jill: I'll take it! Give it to me! I need a desk chair.

Eric: Hm....I can give it to you for $40.

Jill: $40! That's expensive. A new chair _____(4)_____ $40 at the Superstore. How _____(5)_____ $20?

Eric: $20? I _____(6)_____ $50 for it.

Jill: How long have you had it for?

Eric: I've had it for two years, but it is in _____(7)_____ condition. And it's a very lucky chair.

Tom: How is it _____(8)_____?

Eric: I've studied for all my tests sitting in this chair. I always get A's on all my tests.

Tom: That is lucky. Would you _____(9)_____ $30?

Jill: Tom! I want the chair. I'll give you $35.

Eric: Wait. So Tom, you'll buy it for $30? And Jill, you want it for $35?

Tom: I'll give you $40!

Jill: I'll take it for _____(10)_____.

Tom: $41

Jill: $42.50.

Tom: $55! And that's my _____(11)_____ offer!

Jill: Wow, that's _____(12)_____ for a used chair! Eric paid $50 for it.

Tom: Hm...You're right.

Eric: _____(13)_____ to Tom for $55! Take care of my lucky chair, Tom.

Jill: Wait. Why are you _____(14)_____ it in the first place, if it's lucky?

Eric: My friend has a chair and he's always gotten A pluses. I'm _____(15)_____ his lucky chair.

Lessons 21-24: Grammar A

SHOPPING

Adverbs of frequency

We often use adverbs of frequency with the simple present.
I **rarely** buy newspapers. We **often** buy magazines.
100%　　　　　　　　50%　　　　　　　　　　　　　　　　　0% always　usually　often　sometimes　not often　hardly ever　rarely　never
Adverbs of frequency go before the main verb but after the **BE** verb.
They **rarely** <u>go out</u> at night.　　　　　They <u>are</u> **rarely** out at night. I **always** <u>run</u> after class.　　　　　　I <u>am</u> **always** running to class.
Negative adverbs (seldom, rarely, hardly ever, never) are not used with a negative verb.
Some people ~~don't~~ **never** buy books.　→　Some people **never** buy books.
Adverbs of frequency usually come directly after the **subject** in questions.
Do you **often** buy flowers here? Does she **sometimes** read newspapers?
Ever is used in questions about frequency. **Ever** means "at any time."
Does Mike **ever** buy books?　　　　　Yes, he sometimes buys books.
Ever is not used in affirmative statements.
Mike ~~ever~~ buys books.　→　Mike **never** buys books.

Part 1

Write *C* if the sentence is correct. Write *I* if the sentence is incorrect. Rewrite the incorrect sentences.

1. __I__   I ever buy newspapers.   __I never buy newspapers_____.
2. _____   We don't rarely buy comic books. _____.
3. _____   Jason doesn't ever shop at the mall. _____.
4. _____   We don't never visit the museum. _____.
5. _____   Lena doesn't seldom go to the outdoor market. _____.

Part 2

Write the word in parentheses in the correct location.

1. Janet ___sometimes___ reads _____ magazines. (sometimes)
2. Mark _____ is _____ at the café. (rarely)
3. Do you _____ buy _____ flowers here? (often)
4. Does Gina _____ read _____ things online? (ever)
5. It _____ is _____ quiet at the library. (usually)
6. We _____ buy _____ used things. (hardly ever)

Lessons 21-24: Grammar B

SHOPPING

Modal auxiliaries

> **Modal auxiliaries** go with another **verb** and add to the meaning of the verb.
>
> - She **goes** to the store.
> - She **can't go** to the store now.
> - She **will go** to the store later.
>
> **Can: ability/requests**
>
> - **Can** you **ski**? (ability)
>   - Yes, I **can**.
>   - No, I **can't (cannot)**.
> - Where **can I get** a cheap computer?
> - You **can go** to the mall.
> - **Can** you **drive** me to the mall? (request)
>
> **Will: future events/requests/expressions of willingness or refusal**
>
> - We **will go** to England someday./We'**ll go** to England someday. (future)
> - We **won't (will not) go** to New York next year.
> - **Will** you **take** $50 for the sofa? (requests)
> - I'**ll give** it to you for $75. (expression of willingness)
> - I **won't give** it to you for $50. (refusal)

Part 1

Complete the sentences. Circle *can* or *will*.

1. I like your new mobile phone. **Can**/**Will** I hold it for a minute?
2. I'm interested in this sofa. **Can/Will** you take $65 for it?
3. Yes, I'd like to go to the concert, but tickets **can/will** cost $100.
4. Is there a place where we **can/will** buy flowers around here?
5. I **can't/won't** drive to the mall because I don't have a car.
6. Mary is a vegetarian, so she **can't/won't** eat any meat at the party.

Part 2

Use the modal meanings and the verbs in parentheses to complete the sentences.

1. Nick loves fashion. He ____**will be**____ a fashion designer someday. (future, *be*)
2. A: Nice phone!   B: Yes, and I _____ great pictures with it, too. (ability, *take*)
3. No, I _____ you to the mall. Take the bus instead. (refusal, *not drive*)
4. I _____ if we have any more cameras in the back of the shop. (willingness, *see*)
5. You _____ this online for a lower price. (ability, *buy*)
6. Dani _____ her camera to the class party next week. (future, *bring*)

Lesson 25: Vocabulary

FOOD

Part 1

How often do you eat these foods? Put the words into the best column for you. In class, talk about your ideas with a partner.

chicken yogurt tofu carrots noodles oranges nuts rice apples beans bread cheese

A lot	Not many/much	Never
_____	_____	_____
_____	_____	_____
_____	_____	_____
_____	_____	_____
_____	_____	_____
_____	_____	_____
_____	_____	_____
_____	_____	_____

Part 2

In each conversation, one word is wrong. Cross it out and write the correct word on the line. In class, practice the correct conversations with your partner.

1. A: Do you eat ~~many~~ chicken?
   B: Yes, I love it.
   _____much_____

2. A: Do you eat a lot of carrots?
   B: No, I don't eat a lots of carrots.
   _____

3. A: Do you eat a lot of noodle?
   B: Yes, I eat them all the time.
   _____

4. A: Do you eat much rices?
   B: No, I don't.
   _____

5. A: Do you eat a lot of bread?
   B: No, I don't eat many bread.
   _____

6. A: Do you eat a lot of cheese?
   B: Cheese? I eat it all the times.
   _____

Part 3

Look at B's answers in Part 2. Do you have the same (S) answer or different (D) answers for each question?

1. _____   2. _____   3. _____   4. _____   5. _____   6. _____

Lesson 25: Reading & Writing

FOOD

Part 1

Read the leaflet below.

Do you eat enough vegetables?

Now there is a new, easy way to make sure you are eating enough of all the right foods. It's called MyPlate because it looks like a plate and cup. The plate has four colors: red for fruits, green for vegetables, orange for grains, and purple for proteins. The cup is blue, for dairy. The size of the color piece helps people quickly understand how much of each kind of food they should eat. For example, together the red and green pieces fill half of the plate, but the vegetable piece is bigger. Also, the orange piece is bigger than the purple piece, but together they fill the other half of the plate. Dairy is a cup, not a plate, because milk is one of the main sources of dairy.

Complete the sentences.

1. MyPlate is a chart to help people eat _____.
2. According to the new chart, we should eat more _____ than fruits.
3. Dairy is a cup because _____.
4. According to the new chart, we should eat more _____ than protein.
5. Half of our food should be _____ and _____.

PAIR WORK Discuss the questions.

Compare what you eat with MyPlate. Are there foods you need to eat more often? Do you think the new chart is easy to understand?

Part 2

Imagine your class is going to teach other people about MyPlate. Make a chart that talks about what kinds of food are in each group.

Part 3

Share your chart with a partner. Did you write about the same foods for each category?

Lesson 26: Vocabulary

FOOD

Part 1
Look at the first part of the recipes for two dishes. Put the words below into the correct column.

| butter | salt | oil | tomatoes | flour | onions | pepper | eggs | olives |

In neither	In both	In only one
_____	_____	_____
_____	_____	_____
_____	_____	_____
_____	_____	_____
_____	_____	_____

Chocolate Chip Cookies
1 C. butter
1 1/2 C. sugar
2 eggs
2 t. vanilla
2 C. flour
2/3 C. cocoa powder
3/4 t. baking soda
1/4 t. salt
2 C. chocolate chips

Spanish Potato Omelet
1/2 C. oil
4 potatoes
Little salt
Little pepper
1 large onion
4 eggs
2 tomatoes

Part 2

1. Think about one of your favorite dishes. What is it?
   _____

2. Write the ingredients from Part 1 that are probably in it. In class, tell your partner about the dish.

   _____   _____   _____
   _____   _____   _____
   _____   _____   _____

Part 3
Imagine you want to make the dish in Part 2. Which ingredients do you need to buy?

   _____   _____
   _____   _____

Lesson 26: Reading & Writing

FOOD

Part 1

Read the note and order form.

Fresh from the Farmer

Name: The Jones Family   ORDER FORM

Quantity	Item	Price per item	Total price for item
4	onions	$.50 each	2.00
2	potatoes	$5/bag	10.00
3	tomatoes	$1.50 each	4.50
1	eggs	$3/pack of 12	3.00
1	apples	$4/bag	4.00
		shipping	15.00
		Total	

Rich,
This weekend I want to make fish with a tomato salad and baked potatoes. I have the fish, but I think we need onions. I also want to make an apple pie. Can you send the order to the store?
Sue

Complete the sentences.

1. The Jones family needs some *onions/fish*.
2. *Sue/Rich* probably filled in the order form.
3. The store doesn't sell *grains/fruits*.
4. The total is *$21.50/$38.50*.
5. This store probably doesn't sell *salt/carrots*.

PAIR WORK Talk about why people order food instead of going to the store to buy it.

Part 2

Imagine you want to cook your favorite food but you need some things. Write a text asking your friend to buy them for you.

Part 3

With a partner, talk about what you decided to cook. Do you prefer to eat at home or in a restaurant? Which one is cheaper?

Lesson 27: Vocabulary

FOOD

Part 1

Unscramble each of the things people eat and drink.

1. _____ ecaerl
2. _____ aydnc
3. _____ aotpto ihspc
4. _____ eadrb
5. _____ ecir
6. _____ hteccaloo
7. _____ rtuif
8. _____ saod
9. _____ ajm
10. _____ aadls
11. _____ hknecic
12. _____ astot
13. _____ effoec
14. _____ ebaeletgvs
15. _____ uecij
16. _____ akec
17. _____ ntus
18. _____ iedc eta

Part 2

Do you eat the foods in Part 1? When do you eat them? Put them in the diagram. Add one or two more things to each one of the groups. In class, with your partner talk about your answers.

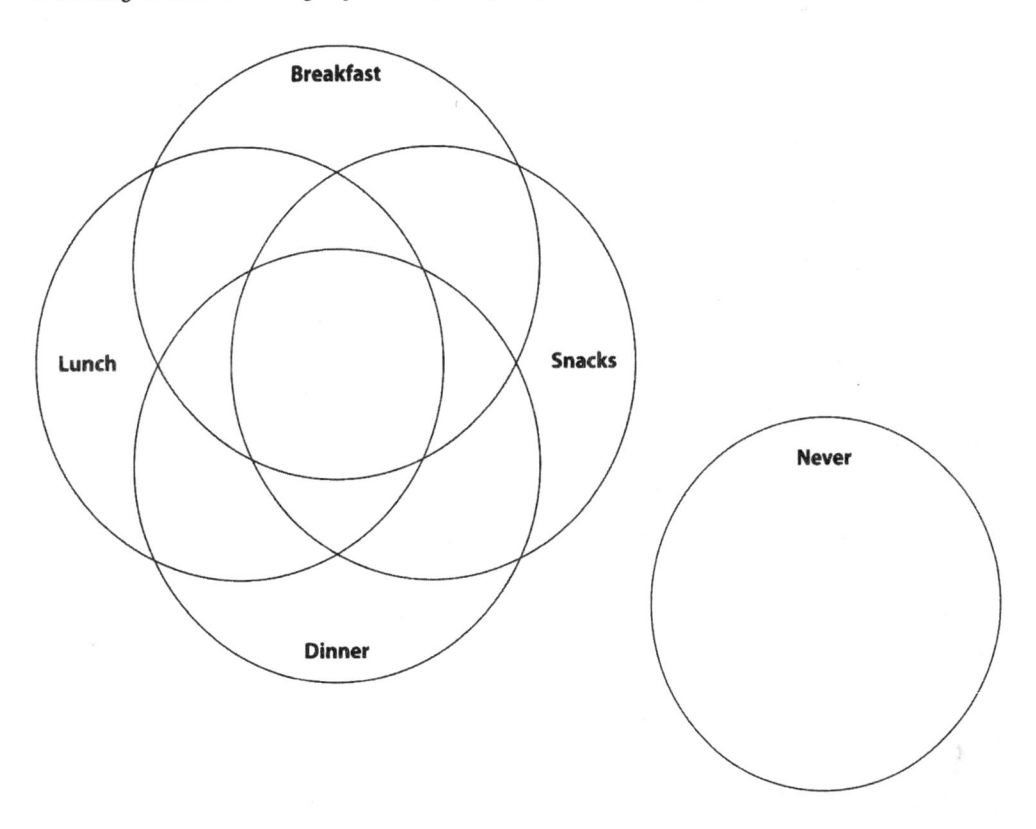

Breakfast

Lunch

Snacks

Dinner

Never

75

Lesson 27: Reading & Writing

FOOD

Part 1

Look at Carrie's Café menu.

Carrie's Café

Breakfast
- toast with jam
- 2 eggs, cooked any way you like
- hot cereal with dried fruit and nuts
- cold cereal

Meals
- grilled cheese sandwich with potato chips
- chicken with baked potato
- paella

Dessert
- chocolate, apple, or honey cake
- strawberry, vanilla, or chocolate ice cream
- yogurt with fruit

Drinks
- soda
- coffee
- apple, orange, or grape juice

Breakfast served all day.
All meals come with hot bread and butter and a choice of soup or salad.

Mark the statements **T** (True) or **F** (False).

_____ 1. At Carrie's Café, you can only eat breakfast in the morning.

_____ 2. The healthiest dessert is the apple cake.

_____ 3. Carrie's Café has lemon juice.

_____ 4. You get a soup and salad with each meal.

_____ 5. There are more breakfast choices than dessert choices.

PAIR WORK Correct the false statements with your partner.

Part 2

Imagine you are going to open a new restaurant. Make a menu using the categories above.

Part 3

Show the menu for your new restaurant to a partner. Take your partner's order. Make suggestions.

Lesson 28: Vocabulary

FOOD

Part 1

Put the words into the correct place in the puzzle.

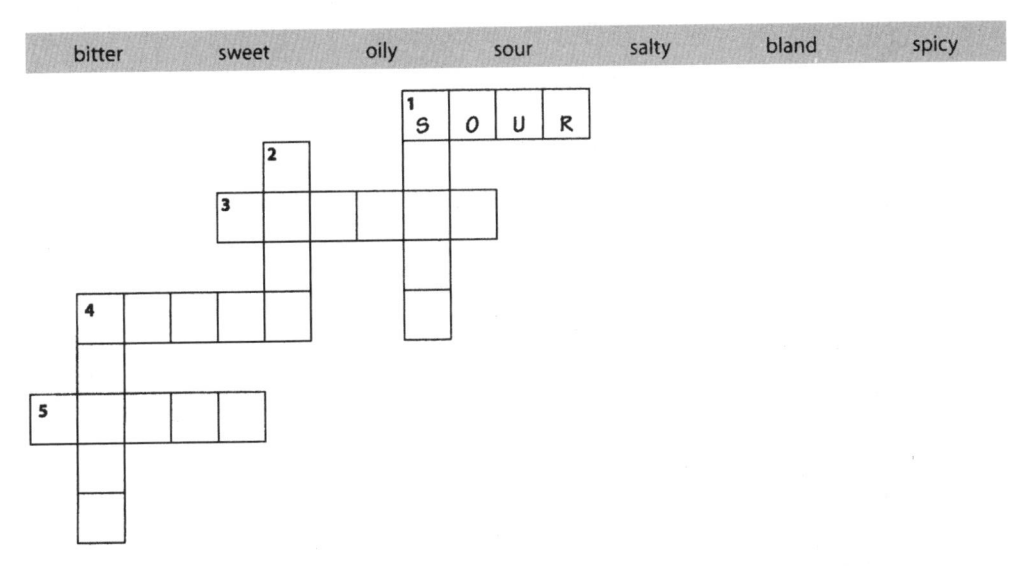

bitter   sweet   oily   sour   salty   bland   spicy

				1 S	O	U	R

(crossword grid with 1 Across = SOUR)

Part 2

Write a clue for each word. In class, compare answers with a partner.

Across

1. _____
3. _____
4. _____
5. _____

Down

1. _____
2. _____
4. _____

Part 3

Which tastes do you like? Write them in order from like the most to like the least. In class, talk about your ideas with a partner.

_____
_____

Lesson 28: Reading & Writing

FOOD

Part 1

Read the fax below.

Pizza Pizza

Subject: Your recent visit   Date: Friday, November 15, 2013
To: Kit Cambridge   From: Claire Yoo, General Manager
Fax: 781-452-6032   Fax: 781-452-8000

Dear Ms. Cambridge,

Thank you for eating at Pizza Pizza two days ago. The evening manager said you thought the food wasn't very good. I am very sorry to hear this. Could you please take a few minutes to answer the questions below and tell us what the problems were?

How did the hot bread taste?

What adjectives would you use to describe the pizza you ate?

What ingredients would you like on a pizza?

Would you eat spaghetti the next time you visit us?

Was any of your food bland?

Please fax your answer to me at the above fax number. We would like to give you a free dinner the next time you visit us.

Thank you for your time,

Claire Yoo

Circle the correct word to complete the sentence.

1. Kit ate pizza on *Wednesday/Friday*.

2. Claire *works/ate* at Pizza Pizza.

3. Kit thought the food was *good/bad*.

4. Kit ate *bread/spaghetti*.

5. Claire wants Kit to *fax/e-mail* her answers.

PAIR WORK Talk about a time when you went to a restaurant and there was a problem (or imagine a situation). What did you do? Would you try the restaurant again?

Part 2

Imagine you are Kit. Write a fax to answer the questions.

Part 3

In pairs, role-play the situation. Student A reads the answers to Claire's questions. Student B is the Pizza Pizza General Manager and replies to each response.

Lessons 25-28: Video Cloze

FOOD

Watch *Tom Cooks Dinner* and fill in the blanks.

Eric: What time are Maria and Jill coming over?
Tom: I told them to come by around 7:00.
Eric: It's almost 7:00. Do you want me to help cook?
Tom: No, it's OK. You know I love to cook.
Eric: OK. What are you _____(1)_____ to make?
Tom: I'm not sure.
Eric: No _____(2)_____, right? We had pasta every day for the past few weeks.
Tom: OK, no pasta.
Eric: What about _____(3)_____ and rice?
Tom: What are the ingredients?
Eric: Hm. Potatoes, _____(4)_____, carrots, coconut milk, and rice. Oh, and lots of spices. It's spicy, but it's _____(5)_____.
Tom: OK, let's see what we have.
Eric: What do we need to buy?
Tom: We need some onions...
Eric: Do we need to get any _____(6)_____?
Tom: No, we have some potatoes. But we need _____(7)_____, coconut milk, rice, and lots of spices.
Eric: We don't have time to go to the supermarket.
Tom: We can make something with what we have.
Eric: That must be them. Come in!
Jill: Hi Eric! Hi Tom!

Eric/Tom: Hello. Hi!
Maria: Thank you so much for _____(8)_____ us to dinner!
Tom: No problem.
Maria: What are you guys cooking for dinner?
Tom: We're not sure. Do you guys eat many _____(9)_____?
Jill: Yes, I eat vegetables _____(10)_____ day.
Maria: Actually, I never eat vegetables. I don't like them.
Tom: Hm. OK. What about _____(11)_____?
Maria: I _____(12)_____ eat chicken.
Jill: I try not to eat a lot of _____(13)_____.
Tom: What about potatoes?
Jill/Maria: We both don't eat potatoes.
Tom: Hm... OK, I think I know what to make. We have everything we need and I know everyone's going to like it.
Jill: What is it?
Tom: I can't tell you. It's a surprise.
Maria: What's it taste like?
Tom: Not too _____(14)_____ and not too _____(15)_____. It's delicious.
Eric: What's in it?
Tom: Tomatoes, cheese, noodles...
Eric/Jill/Maria: Pasta!
Tom: That's right! How did you guys know?
Eric: Pasta.

79

Lessons 25-28: Grammar

FOOD

Count and noncount nouns

Count nouns can be singular or plural.		Noncount nouns can only be singular.	
an apple	**a few** apples	cheese	water
a cup	**some** cups	**some** broccoli	**some** coffee
one potato chip	**two** potato chips	**a little** salt	**a lot of** pepper
one person	**a lot of** people	**a bowl of** rice	**two cups of** flour
Individual items are often count nouns. The group or category they belong to is often a noncount noun.			
Count (item)	**Noncount (category)**	**Count (item)**	**Noncount (category)**
banana		table	
oranges →	fruit	chairs →	furniture
apples		desks	
Use **many** and **how many** in questions with count nouns.		Use **much** and **how much** in questions with noncount nouns.	
Do you eat **many vegetables**?		Do you eat **much spinach**?	
How many slices of pizza do you want?		**How much pizza** do you want?	

Part 1

Complete the shopping list with *a few* or *a little*.

We need

1. _____a few_____ oranges
2. _____ rice
3. _____ bottles of water
4. _____ flour
5. _____ coffee
6. _____ eggs
7. _____ onions
8. _____ milk

Part 2

Complete the sentences. Circle the best word.

1. Do you eat **much/many** protein?
2. How **much/many** carrots do you want?
3. I eat a lot of **nut/nuts**.
4. Do you drink a lot of **water/waters**?
5. We don't have **much/many** coffee left.
6. The soup needs **a little/a few** salt.
7. Do you need **much/many** eggs for this recipe?
8. How **much/many** slices of cake do you want?

Lesson 29: Vocabulary

PAST & FUTURE

Part 1

Use the words in parentheses to write sentences with information that is true for you.

1. _____ last weekend. (study)
2. _____ all day yesterday. (stay home)
3. _____ last night. (meet friends)
4. _____ last weekend. (go shopping)
5. _____ last Saturday. (see a movie)
6. _____ the day before yesterday. (get a haircut)

In class, compare answers with a partner. Ask follow-up questions.

A: Did you study last weekend?
B: No, I didn't. I went shopping and had dinner with a friend.
A: Where did you eat?

Part 2

In each conversation, there is a mistake. Cross it out and write the correct word on the line. In class, practice the correct conversations with your partner.

1. A: How ~~did~~ your weekend?
   B: It was great.
   _____was_____

2. A: Did you went shopping?
   B: No, I didn't.
   _____

3. A: How about you?
   B: I did stay home all day on Saturday.
   _____

4. A: My weekend was OK.
   B: What did you doing?
   _____

5. A: What about you? What did you do?
   B: I was watching a movie.
   _____

6. A: Did you do anything special on Friday?
   B: Not really. I didn't go shopping. and I didn't watched any movies.
   _____

Lesson 29: Reading & Writing

PAST & FUTURE

Part 1

Read the e-mail below.

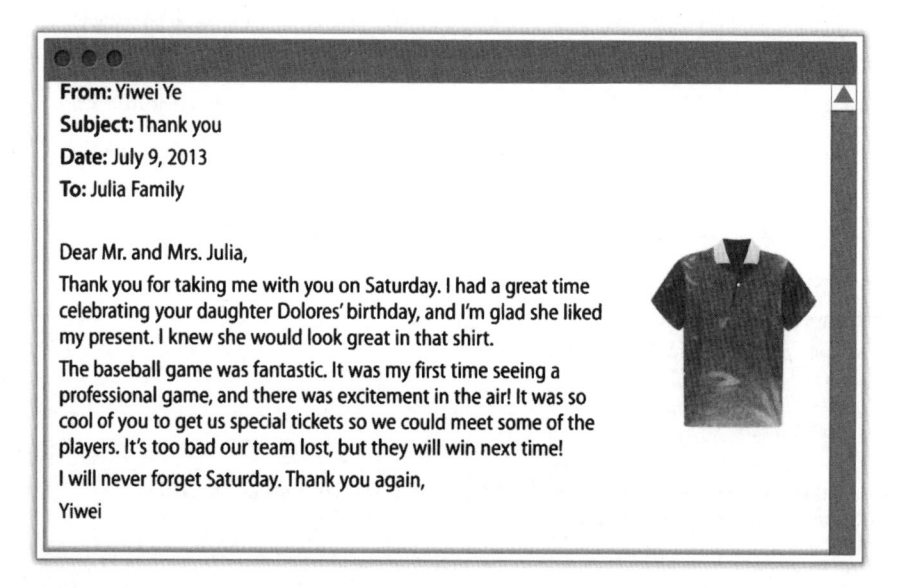

From: Yiwei Ye
Subject: Thank you
Date: July 9, 2013
To: Julia Family

Dear Mr. and Mrs. Julia,

Thank you for taking me with you on Saturday. I had a great time celebrating your daughter Dolores' birthday, and I'm glad she liked my present. I knew she would look great in that shirt.

The baseball game was fantastic. It was my first time seeing a professional game, and there was excitement in the air! It was so cool of you to get us special tickets so we could meet some of the players. It's too bad our team lost, but they will win next time!

I will never forget Saturday. Thank you again,

Yiwei

Complete the sentences.

1. Yiwei gave Dolores a present for her _____.
2. Dolores' last name is _____.
3. Yiwei's present was a _____.
4. The team Mr. and Mrs. Julia like _____ the game.
5. They got to meet _____.
6. It was the first time Yiwei saw _____.

PAIR WORK Discuss the questions.

1. How would you feel if you were Yiwei?
2. What do people usually do to celebrate birthdays in your country?
3. What sports and events are popular to watch in your country?
4. In your country, when do people usually write thank you letters?

Part 2

Imagine someone took you to a special event. Write an e-mail to thank the person.

Part 3

Share your thank you e-mail with your classmates. Is there a special event someone wrote about that you want to go to? As a class, pick the top five special events.

Lesson 30: Vocabulary

PAST & FUTURE

Part 1

Complete the sentences with information that is true for you.

1. _____ last month.
2. _____ yesterday afternoon.
3. _____ yesterday morning.
4. _____ last week.
5. _____ last year.
6. _____ the day before yesterday.
7. _____ last night.
8. _____ this morning.

In class, compare answers with a partner.

A: What did you do last month?
B: I went to that new movie with George Clooney. It was great.

Part 2

Complete the sentences with past time expressions from Part 1. You can use the expressions more than once. In class, compare answers with a partner.

1. I studied _____.
2. I _____ friends _____.
3. I _____ a movie _____.
4. I _____ a haircut _____.
5. I _____ shopping _____.
6. I _____ out to eat _____.
7. I _____ a walk _____.
8. I _____ a shower _____.
9. I _____ e-mail _____.
10. I _____ to bed _____.
11. I _____ up early _____.
12. I _____ dinner _____.

Lesson 30: Reading & Writing

PAST & FUTURE

Part 1

Read the memo.

While you were out...

To: Professor Julie Davis
Date: July 15, 2013   Time: 8:30 a.m.
~~Mr.~~/Ms. Judy Birch   of Birmingham Language Schools
Phone: 402-485-0123   ext: 7982

✓ telephoned   ___ urgent
___ will call again   ✓ please call
✓ wants to see you   ___ returned your call

Message: She said she called yesterday afternoon, too, between 4 p.m. and 5 p.m. I didn't talk to her. Did you get the message? She wants to talk to you about next year's classes. She said she received the class schedule that you sent but there are some problems. She wants you to call today, and she wants to meet you tomorrow.
Sally

Complete the sentences.

1. _____ called yesterday and today.
2. Ms. Birch works at _____.
3. Professor Davis sent _____ to Ms. Birch.
4. _____ wrote the memo.
5. Professor Davis and Ms. Birch will probably meet _____.

PAIR WORK Discuss the questions.

Do you think Ms. Birch called too soon after the first call? What do you think about Professor Davis not calling back after the first call?

Part 2

Imagine Ms. Birch sent an e-mail instead of calling on July 15. Use the information from the memo to write the e-mail.

Part 3

In pairs, compare your e-mail with a partner's. Do you ask why Professor Davis did not return your call? How do you think Professor Davis will respond to this e-mail?

Lesson 31: Vocabulary

PAST & FUTURE

Part 1

Unscramble each of the words used to react to news.

1. _____ cyras
2. _____ waluf
3. _____ nsattafci
4. _____ beleirrt
5. _____ dbielcreni
6. _____ gxiintce
7. _____ nusoregad
8. _____ zaimgna

Part 2

Use each of the words in Part 1 once and complete the conversations. In class, practice the conversations with a partner.

1.

A: How was the test?

B: _____

A: Why? You studied all week.

B: I know, but it was _____. It was really hard!

2.

A: How was snowboarding? Did you like it?

B: Well, it was kind of _____, but it was too _____. I don't think I'll go again.

3.

A: How was your trip?

B: It was _____. The food was _____, and the people were _____. They helped me every time I got lost. I want to go back again!

4.

A: You won't believe this! I just went bungee jumping! It was great!

B: It sounds _____ to me. I don't think I'll try!

Lesson 31: Reading & Writing

PAST & FUTURE

Part 1

Read the magazine article.

Twice in the same day

Winning the lottery is amazingly lucky. But winning the lottery two times in the same day? Very few people can tell you what that feels like, but A.V. in the United States can.

She was in the hospital taking care of her mother when she saw the winning numbers on a TV news show. She looked at her mom and said, "You won't believe this! I won! Twice!" All she could say was, "Incredible!"

"When A.V. called me, she said, 'Listen to this. I won the lottery—twice!' But I thought she was joking," her friend, S.J., said.

She had chosen numbers related to her parents' ages and the year they were married. When asked what she was going to do with the money, she said she was looking forward to taking care of her parents.

Answer the questions.

1. Who is the *she* that says "Incredible"? _____
2. Why is A.V. unusual? _____
3. How is A.V. going to use the money? _____
4. Where was A.V. when she heard she won? _____
5. Who thought A.V. didn't really win the lottery? _____

PAIR WORK Discuss the questions.

1. What would you do if you won a lot of money?
2. Would you rather win money or a trip? Why?
3. What are some other experiences that make people say, "You won't believe this"?

Part 2

Imagine that something exciting happened to you. Write a short magazine article talking about your experience.

Part 3

In groups of four, take turns reading your magazine articles. For which stories would you say, "I thought she/he was joking," because it's so incredible?

Lesson 32: Vocabulary

PAST & FUTURE

Part 1

Write one or two words to complete each activity. If a word is not needed, write an X. Then match each activity to its meaning.

1. _____ for a test
2. _____ up late
3. _____ the mall
4. _____ out of town
5. _____ watch sports
6. _____ to a park
7. _____ relatives
8. _____ a museum

A. go see people who are your family
B. go to a place outside to play
C. watch people play games
D. go to a place to see beautiful pictures
E. go to a place where you can shop
F. go to another city
G. not go to bed early
H. study before a test

Part 2

How often do you do the activities in Part 1? Write the six activities you do the most often. Put them in order from most often to least often. In class, talk about your ideas with a partner.

_____

_____

Part 3

Complete the conversations with your own plans. In class, practice the conversations with a partner.

1.

Mo Lin: What are your plans for tonight?

You: _____.

2.

Massimo: What are you going to do after class?

You: _____.

3.

Collin: What are you doing tomorrow night?

You: _____.

4.

Max: Are you doing anything fun this weekend?

You: _____.

Lesson 32: Reading & Writing

PAST & FUTURE

Part 1

Read the notice below.

Summer classes

Summer vacation starts May 24. What are your plans? Why not use your summer to learn something exciting? You will get school credit to have fun.

Golf

Summer is the perfect time to learn golf, and golf is a skill that can help you in business in the future.

$230 for class and all golf games. Class meets every weekday morning, 8 a.m., at the Field Crest Golf Club on Irving Drive during the month of June.

Rock Climbing

Learn how to enjoy this challenging sport while staying safe.

$100. All students must have a helmet, which is not included in the fee. Class meets at the rock climbing wall in the school gym every Saturday in August, 8 a.m. to 11 a.m.

Contact Mr. Price if you want to take either of these classes.

Answer the questions.

1. Could a student take both classes? _____
2. For which class do students need to buy a helmet? _____
3. If a student lives next to the university, which class would be closer to go to? _____
4. According to the notice, which sport might be good for marketing students to learn? _____
5. Which starts first, summer vacation or the golf classes? _____

PAIR WORK Discuss the questions.

1. If you had to take one of the classes, which one would you choose? Why?
2. What do you think about taking classes during the summer vacation?

Part 2

Imagine you are going to take one of the classes. Write an e-mail telling your friend about the class and how you feel before the class starts.

Part 3

Share your feelings and the e-mail with a partner Why do you feel this way? If you could take any kind of adventure or sports class, what would it be? Share your answers.

Lessons 29-32: Video Cloze

PAST & FUTURE

Watch *Jill's Trip* and fill in the blanks.

Eric: Hi, Jill.
Jill: Hi, Eric.
Eric: How's it going? How was your _____(1) in Washington, D.C.?
Jill: _____(2)! It was really a _____(3) time.
Eric: Oh yeah? What did you do there?
Jill: Well, first, I _____(4) a bus tour of the city. It really is such a beautiful place - so many _____(5) buildings and monuments. I love the Washington Monument.
Eric: Yeah. The monument is _____(6).
Jill: Then I went to the Smithsonian Museum. There's always so much stuff to see there.
Eric: Yeah, I _____(7) a great dinosaur exhibition the last time I was there. It was fantastic.
Jill: Wow! After that I decided to walk to the Lincoln Memorial, but then it started to rain and I got completely wet.
Eric: How _____(8)!
Jill: No, it was OK. I went back to my hotel, changed my clothes, and went out again later, this time with an umbrella!
Eric: Good thinking.
Jill: That night, I went to a classical concert. How about you? What _____(9) you do last weekend?

Eric: Not much really. I worked all day on Saturday. On Sunday, Tom and I _____(10) tennis.
Jill: Oh, you exercised!
Eric: Yep. After that we _____(11) to a movie. We saw the new James Bond film.
Jill: You did? How was it?
Eric: It was great! Then we went shopping.
Jill: Did you buy anything?
Eric: Yeah, I _____(12) this video camera. It was $500, but I got it on sale for only $175. You won't _____(13) what I got on this video camera.
Jill: What?
Eric: I was at the park, and I saw an elephant!
Jill: No way! Why was the elephant in the park?
Eric: It had _____(14) from the zoo! It wasn't dangerous. I even gave it my sandwich. It was incredible, and I have it all on video. I'm going to put it on YouTube.
Jill: Oh! I want to see!
Eric: Hold on...
Tom: Hello? Hellooooo?
Tom: Hello! Hi Eric! This is a really nice camera. I just _____(15) to tell you that. I hope I didn't erase anything important.

Lessons 29-32: Grammar A

PAST & FUTURE

Simple past tense

> The **simple past tense** expresses a past action that is finished. There is only one form of the past tense for all persons.

Last night we **went** to the movies. Marie **came** with us. I **stayed** up pretty late.

Spelling Rules
For regular verbs, the simple past tense is formed by adding **-d** or **-ed**.
like → like**d**   name → name**d**   **pass** → pass**ed**   want → want**ed**
If a verb has only one syllable and ends in **one vowel + one consonant**, double the consonant and add **-ed**.
plan → plan**ned**   stop → stop**ped**
If a verb ends in a **consonant + -y**, drop the y and add **-ied**.
study → stud**ied**   carry → carr**ied**

Some Irregular Past Tense Verbs			
buy **bought**	get **got**	see **saw**	take **took**
come **came**	go **went**	pay **paid**	think **thought**
drink **drank**	have **had**	say **said**	wear **wore**
eat **ate**	make **made**	sit **sat**	write **wrote**

Complete the sentences with the simple past forms of the verbs in parentheses.

1. Last weekend, I ____**stayed**____ home. (stay)
2. Rob and Mary _____ at the library last night. (study)
3. Mike's tired! He _____ all day yesterday. (work)
4. We _____ to a great concert last weekend! (go)
5. Peter _____ the new Johnny Depp movie yesterday. (see)
6. Rick _____ his friends to the beach last Sunday. (take)
7. I _____ to visit to my family last week, but I'm going this week instead. (plan)
8. We were going to go hiking last Saturday, but it _____. (rain)
9. We _____ a lot of popcorn during the movie! (eat)
10. We _____ in the front row at the movie last night. (sit)
11. It _____ hot yesterday! (be)
12. We _____ a lot of water during the soccer game. (drink)
13. Sandy _____ her homework just before class. (finish)
14. Alan looks great! He _____ a haircut yesterday. (get)
15. Jason _____ a lot of new clothes at the mall last night. (buy)

Lessons 29-32: Grammar B

PAST & FUTURE

Future time

Future time can be expressed by using *going to* with a verb.					
Next year, **I am going to have** my own apartment. Jill **is going to see** a movie this weekend.					
Affirmative					
I	am	going to	eat	at 7 p.m.	
He/She/It	is				
We/You/They	are				
Negative					
I	am	not	going to	watch	the game this weekend.
He/She/It	is				
We/You/They	are				
Yes/No Questions					
Am	I	going to	see	a movie tomorrow?	
Is	he/she/it				
Are	we/you/they				
Information Questions					
How	am	I	going to	get	home?
What	is	he/she/it		do	next?
When	are	we/you/they		eat	lunch?

Complete the sentences with the BE verb, *going to*, and the verb in parentheses.

1. What __are__ Rex and Amy __going to do__ this weekend? (do)
2. _____ Max _____ a movie with us tonight? (see)
3. Alan _____ to the museum this weekend. (go)
4. Sylvia _____ home next Saturday. (not stay)
5. We _____ the game on TV this weekend. (not watch)
6. Where _____ you _____ after school today? (go)
7. _____ we _____ to dinner tomorrow night? (go out)
8. When _____ Julie _____ shopping? (go)
9. Marta _____ at the library after class. (not study)
10. How _____ Rick _____ to the game this weekend? (get)
11. Steve and Jamie _____ a picnic in the park this weekend. (have)
12. _____ Dave and Karen _____ with us tonight? (come)